The New
Self-Hypnosis

Dr. Paul T. Adams

Melvin Powers
Wilshire Book Company

12015 Sherman Road, No. Hollywood, CA 91605

LIBRARY OF CONGRESS
CATALOG CARD NUMBER: 67-16377

*All names mentioned in the cases of this book are
fictitious and have no reference to anyone living
or dead. The cases are real. The names have been
changed to protect the identity of those involved.*

PRINTED IN THE UNITED STATES OF AMERICA

ISBN 0-87980-233-2

A MEDICAL DOCTOR'S FOREWORD

Dr. Paul T. Adams has written a new book on self-hypnosis, a wonderfully practical book that outlines the techniques necessary to master self-hypnosis easily, correctly, and safely. He is especially qualified to do this because of his vast knowledge of psychology and religion, together with his excellent background of training and experience in hypnotism for many years. This book, however, is a great deal more than a discussion on self-hypnosis. It is in reality a book on how, in these troubled times, to live, to enrich one's life in hundreds of ways, to begin a new set of habit patterns, and to stick to them by means of hypnotism.

As a brilliant and fearless leader, Dr. Adams challenges each individual to lead a spiritually rewarding life and then shows the reader how to do it effortlessly by self-hypnosis.

As an experienced and effective counsellor, Dr. Adams enables the reader to meet these spiritual challenges by showing how to locate the "weeds" in one's "garden of thought" and hoe them out by a new and dynamic self-hypnotic process.

Having been the first medical doctor to specialize in the use of hypnosis in the United States, I know better than most the difficulties of applying self-hypnosis. I believe that Dr. Adams has written a very clear and understandable book which takes the mystery out of the phenomenon.

Each and every reader will find a practical use for this book. It is certain to be of outstanding service as real self-help to anyone interested in the realistic field of hypnotism.

WILLIAM J. BRYAN, JR., M.D.

THIS BOOK IS DEDICATED TO MY BELOVED WIFE, BETTY,
AND TO MY FOUR P.D.E.M'S—
PAUL II, BLAIR, BRADFORD, AND PERRY

WHAT THIS BOOK CAN DO FOR YOU

THIS BOOK IS NOT JUST another book about self-hypnosis. The individual who has no interest whatsoever in hypnotism will, nevertheless, find it of great value and interest. Section III of this book comes to grips with the problems of life which confront us all. Unique insight into the difficulties of living in this modern space age is presented in a manner which is direct and understandable, and step-by-step ways of solving these problems are given. The instructions found in this book are the result of many years of counseling people who experience difficulty in meeting the demands of the space age.

If you are interested in self-hypnosis, you will find sections I and II to be most refreshing. You won't find a lot of hashed-over ideas. *The approach to the subject of hypnosis is different from anything yet written.* Dr. Adams explains what hypnosis is and how it works. Then he gives nine different suggestion tests, which you can try on yourself. Next, you are given pointed instruction on how you can actually hypnotize yourself. Word for word inductions are presented, so that even the most uninformed individual can be successful in learning self-hypnosis.

Dr. Adams simply and yet thoroughly explains how the subconscious functions. The part the imagination plays in hypnosis is dealt with lucidly. Chapter 9 is indeed unique and unusual, for in it you will find six principles which can be used in self-hypnosis suggestions. Dr. Adams contends that what you tell yourself while under hypnosis is more important than the depth of your hypnosis. *Chapter 9 also contains the secret of your P.D.E.M., referred to throughout the book.*

The material found in Sections I and II is the result of Dr. Adams' group courses on self-hypnosis. People from all walks of life and from divergent religious backgrounds have taken this course. Besides pastoring a large congregation, giving private counsel, teaching group courses, writing, and lecturing, Dr. Adams serves as a consultant to a number of industrial and sales firms. His advice is sought by these firms on matters of human relations and motivations.

All in all, you will find reading this book an enriching experience. You will find yourself referring to it often for guidance, and for practical direction in leading a more fulfilled life of health, wealth, and happiness.

CONTENTS

Section Three

THE RE-EDUCATION

AUTHOR'S INTRODUCTION

A WISE MAN MANY CENTURIES ago wrote: "For as a man thinketh in his heart, so is he." (Proverbs 23:7 K.J.V.) If King Solomon were to write this same statement in modern English he would write: "For as a man thinketh in his subconscious or his inner mind, so is he." The word "heart," as used in this Scripture and in most Scriptures of the Hebrew and Christian Testaments, does not refer to your physical heart. Instead it is used figuratively and usually refers to the seat of the emotions, the inner mind of man, the subconscious. Long before Freud was born, King Solomon said that the thing which determines human character and conduct is not what a man thinks or verbalizes consciously, but what he thinks "in his heart," or subconsciously.

Since the time of Solomon many discoveries have been made which confirm his statement. Yet nothing has been discovered which would supersede it. What you think in your heart becomes you. Sometimes this is good and sometimes this is bad, depending on what you think in your subconscious. The tragedy is that many times response patterns are set up in your subconscious of which you are completely unaware. These behavior patterns can ruin you. The failure says, "I don't want to fail," yet he continues to do things which make him fail. The man who suffers from extreme anxiety says, "I don't want to be afraid . . . ," yet he continues to be afraid. Why? Compulsion, anxiety, phobia, obsession, plus scores of other names are given as answers, but the real answer is that the subconscious of such an individual is convinced that these behavior responses are necessary to his life.

How can the subconscious be reached? How can the subconscious be re-educated? I believe the best way is by the proper use of hypnosis and self-hypnosis. Numerous people have been and are being helped to live confidently as they meet the demands of the space age. I hope that through the lessons you learn from this book you will be able to achieve just this.

This book is for everyone, because hypnosis is a gift from God for everyone. If you feel you can't stand any improvement in your life, then you shouldn't bother to read any further. But if you want to live life to the fullest, proceed to do so now, with this book as your dependable friend and guide.

1

SELF-HYPNOSIS—
AN ANCIENT ART
TO MEET THE LIVING NEEDS
OF A MODERN AGE

You will probably shake your head with disbelief when I tell you that you have been hypnotized every day of your life. Even if you don't believe this statement it is, nonetheless, true. In fact, you have not only been hypnotized every day of your life, with the possible exemption of your infant years, but you have, in a certain sense, been hypnotized all of your life. As we proceed you will find both of these statements to be true.

MISCONCEPTIONS

The average person approaches the subject of hypnotism with numerous preconceived ideas, mostly erroneous. These ideas range from believing that hypnosis and sleep are synonymous to believing that a hypnotist possesses some Satanic power. Since I am a minister, I have quite often experienced the last misconception. Well-meaning mothers and fathers warn their children not to look me in the eyes lest I cast a spell over them. Some of the good brethren warn their flocks to avoid me, since it is possible to become "demon-possessed" if they venture too close to me.

3

These examples are a little extreme, but are indicative of the attitudes of a great number of individuals.

Today, as never before, enlightened people are beginning to realize how hypnotism can help them attain their goals and ambitions. Many books have been written and many courses have been given that tell people *what* to do, but none of them tell people *how* to accomplish *what* they are supposed to do. Self-hypnosis is the one dynamic tool that is effective in implementing and putting into operation the plans you have for your life.

HYPNOSIS SHOULD NOT BE FEARED

By the use of hypnosis you can release the power that is within you. Hypnosis is as old as man, yet only a few have availed themselves of its benefits. Fear is the one big reason why men have not and do not use hypnosis. Hypnosis represents a misunderstood power, and men invariably fear anything which is powerful or which they don't understand. Priests and kings in ancient times exercised hypnosis as a divine power. True, they did not call it hypnosis, but this is what it was. They believed God had imparted to them a gift of power over their subjects, but the truth of the matter is they were merely evoking a power which resides in everyone. This power, which resides within every man and has caused him to see visions, hear the unheard, and accomplish the impossible, has been unleashed by hypnosis to make the sick well, the blind see, and the deaf hear.

Men still fear hypnosis because of the phenomena which can be evoked by it: catatonic states, anesthesia, hallucinations . . . Even some of the most sophisticated people cling to the false association of magic and hypnosis. They believe the hypnotist has some mystical, magical power. Nothing could be further from the truth. The hypnotist is merely releasing a power within his subject.

This is a God-given power! It is a power which resides within and which is available to you. It is waiting to be used, governed, and controlled by you.

Any authority on hypnosis will tell you that all hypnosis is self-hypnosis. The hypnotist is merely a guide. He is governing and controlling a force which is within the subject. Once the individual is properly instructed and conditioned, he can govern and control this force himself.

SOURCE OF HYPNOTIC POWER

It is interesting and amazing to me that man's concern for outer space started at approximately the same time he became interested in inner space—hypnosis. In fact, I understand that hypnotic techniques are used on some astronauts to condition them to the many facets of their work.

Have you ever noticed how very successful men seem to be possessed by a power? You, no doubt, have heard someone say Mr. So & So is a man possessed by a Divine Force. In reality, the successful man is not possessed of a power but possesses his own power. This is the potential of every living mortal. Jesus Christ realized this when he stated: "The Kingdom of God is within you." The difference between the man who has reaped the harvest of the good things of this world and the man who hasn't is that one has tapped and controlled the unseen force within himself and the other hasn't.

Hypnosis, hypnotism, and self-hypnosis are only words. Most of the great men and women of the past who effectively used this force knew nothing of hypnosis as we know it today. We still don't know everything about hypnosis. We don't, for example, understand why some people are more easily hypnotized than others, or why some go deeper into hypnosis than others. In short, we don't understand exactly how it works, but we do know that it works, and as far as you and I are concerned this is the most important thing. Constant research is being done concerning the dynamics and mechanisms of hypnotism, but enough is known today so that you may avail yourselves of the benefits of self-hypnosis. You can begin to guide and direct the full potential of your life.

Did you ever stop to analyze what causes one man to succeed and another to fail? This factor is given various names such as: drive, punch, etc. Yet none of these terms begin to adequately define "that certain something" which makes men successful. Two men may be identical in physical stature and mental ability. They may be engaged in the same occupation, yet one will be more successful than the other. Why? To find the real reason, you must go back to the premise that the successful man, even though he knows nothing about hypnosis, possesses, governs, controls, and unleashes the power within himself.

RELEASING FULL POTENTIAL THROUGH HYPNOTISM

The purpose of this book is to teach you how to use self-hypnosis intelligently, so you, too, can realize your full potential in life. In this space age more is expected and demanded from man's mind. A child in the fourth grade is getting mathematics and science which the previous generation received in the eighth or ninth grade. In fact, the average school child today is learning math and science which didn't exist a few years ago.

Industry is becoming more and more stringent in its requirements. Men must have a college degree to obtain the humblest positions. Continuous education is expected of employees in all major firms. In order to stay "on top of the heap" the average executive has to spend hours reading about new advancements and techniques in his particular field. Promotions seldom come to the man who isn't improving himself.

The housewife who wants to stay in step with her husband and children also has many mental demands made of her. Besides all of her household duties, clubs, and church functions, she must find time to keep informed. The wife and mother who doesn't will find that she is soon out of the inner circle of her family. This is one of the reasons for the dissolution of many marriages—the wife doesn't grow intellectually with her husband.

The reverse is also true. Recently, I came into contact with a married couple in their early fifties who were on the verge of separation. The basic difficulty in their marriage was the intellectual difference. The woman was self-educated and had a great many intellectual and cultural interests. Her husband, however, wasn't interested in anything except T.V. and comic strips. He didn't care for any of his wife's friends because he felt out of place. By means of a hypnotic technique I motivated him to take an interest in reading and learning. I taught him self-hypnosis so that he might increase his powers of concentration, comprehension, and memory. It wasn't long until the man became part of a whole new world, and a marriage was saved.

HYPNOSIS IS THE KEY FOR EFFECTIVE LIVING

We have brought to your attention just a few of the mental demands modern society requests of twentieth century space age citizens. Let me ask you a very important question. How will you and your children find it possible to meet these demands? Psychologists believe that the average person uses only eight per cent of his mind power when he engages in serious study. If you doubt this fact, try this little experiment. How much of the last few pages you have read in this book do you remember? Better yet, take a school textbook, read a page or two and examine yourself to see how much you can comprehend. The difficulty will be greatly increased if you use material which you don't particularly like.

The problem is this: How are you going to resuscitate this great reservoir of dormant mind power? To begin with, most unused mind power is classified as subconscious. The best way to reach the subconscious is by a hypnotic technique. Hypnosis and self-hypnosis are the answer to your mental demands. Within a decade or two, self-hypnosis will be used in almost every facet of modern man's life.

If you want to be successful in your life's ambitions, if you want to stay abreast of the times and meet the mental requirements of this age, then it is imperative that you acquire a good working knowledge of self-hypnosis.

There are, of course, some individuals who have no desire to improve themselves. They are satisfied with the status quo. They are content to let the world go by. Whatever the world doles out is good enough for them. Sometimes they actually take pride in the fact that they are ignorant. This is indeed a shame! I take it for granted that you are not this type of individual, or you wouldn't be reading this book.

It is necessary that you do more than merely read this book if you are to learn how to hypnotize yourself. You should reread it a number of times, and you must also practice the things I will teach you. Some of you will learn how to hypnotize yourselves more easily than others, but anyone with a normal mind can learn self-hypnosis and learn it well. Individuals who tell you they have tried and didn't succeed are people who didn't try hard enough and long enough.

In order for you to learn how to hypnotize yourself effectively, you must know something about the mechanisms of hypnosis. You should know at least a little about the history of hypnosis. (There are many good books dealing with this subject.) Knowing how hypnosis works will remove most of your fears, and fear is one of the greatest enemies of hypnosis.

I have noticed in my self-hypnosis classes that when people understand hypnosis and lose their fears, they go into hypnosis very easily. At first, trying too hard may be a hindrance to some of you. Motivation of the right kind is very important, but "over" motivation can be a definite detriment to the achievement of self-hypnosis.

Chronological age has little or nothing to do with learning self-hypnosis, for I believe anyone from twelve years on can achieve it. Some children under twelve even learn this art. In the upper age brackets the only deterrent is senility. As long as an individual has an open mind and a desire to learn self-hypnosis, he can succeed.

As you proceed in the study of self-hypnosis, you will have to unlearn many things. There is no subject more misunderstood than hypnosis. Very, very few educated people are informed about this subject. Men with extensive formal education are just as ignorant concerning hypnosis as the man who can't write his name. Within the next twenty-five years these men will feel embarrassed when they think of the rash statements they have made in regard to the subject of hypnotism.

ESSENTIALS FOR LEARNING SELF-HYPNOSIS

As you approach this new field of study, approach it with a candid, open mind. Don't be like the fellow who knew everything there was to know about math, yet enrolled in a math class. When the teacher asked him why he was taking a math course when he already knew everything there was to know, he replied, "I want to learn some more."

The three essentials for learning self-hypnosis are:

1. A normal mind

2. A desire to learn
3. A program of consistent practice

If you have a normal mind, the proper motivation, and make daily application of what you learn, you will be able to hypnotize yourself.

When I say "hypnotize yourself," I don't mean you will necessarily go into a deep trance or pass out of this world. A great many people are looking for this type of experience. The purpose of this book is to teach you how to learn self-hypnosis constructively for your own personal improvement.

The reason why so few people have succeeded at self-hypnosis on their own is that they don't know what to expect. They don't know whether they have been hypnotized or not.

Remember one thing, even if you forget everything else in this book: There is only one real evidence of true, effective hypnosis, and that is the post-hypnotic response. Post-hypnotic response means that, after you return to a normal state of consciousness, you react to the suggestion you gave yourself while under hypnosis. For example, you hypnotize yourself and, while under hypnosis, you give yourself the suggestion that you will have more patience in dealing with your children. During the relaxation, you might feel hypnotized or you might not feel hypnotized, but if you do develop more patience in regard to your children, that is proof that you were actually under hypnosis.

I am going to go a step further and make a statement which will seem, on the surface, to negate what I have just stated. Some individuals will have to give themselves a suggestion more than once before they get the desired post-hypnotic result. For some unknown cause, some people are naturally more suggestible than others. Those people who are less suggestible must work a little longer to get the post-hypnotic response. The important thing, however, is that it eventually comes. When I work on a certain area of my life with self-hypnosis, I usually allow six weeks before I expect to see the full benefits. Actually six weeks is a very short time to spend in procuring a new habit pattern that will last a life time. Five to fifteen minutes a day for six weeks can sometimes work miracles in your life.

Perhaps I sound overly enthusiastic to you. Note that I said "sometimes." The results are not always the same, but there are always some results, provided the effort is made. What I call a "miracle" might not seem like a miracle to you and vice versa. Twelve-year old George Jenson was brought to my office by his mother. He was already one grade behind and was going to fail again if his marks didn't improve. George was large for his age and had suffered much mental abuse from his classmates. His ego was almost crushed. He was tense, anxious, and lacking in self-confidence. After I analyzed George's problems, it wasn't long before he started to show improvement. I used hypnotic techniques and at the same time taught him self-hypnosis. George passed his grade and passed it well. To me, this is a miracle.

HYPNOSIS AS A PERFECTLY NORMAL PHENOMENON

When I say anyone with a normal mind can learn self-hypnosis I don't mean everyone will go into a deep trance. Actually a deep trance, as far as self-hypnosis is concerned, is detrimental. If you go too deeply into a trance you can't give yourself the proper suggestions.

Self-hypnosis is not something weird and way out. It is practical and constructive. Hypnosis is being used more and more in the field of medicine, but its usefulness doesn't end there. Self-hypnosis can make a positive contribution to almost every area of your life. Physically, it will enable you to be more relaxed at all times and in all situations. This will in no way decrease your efficiency at work, but will serve to increase it. A top rate professional athlete is completely relaxed until a certain amount of energy is needed. For instance, a good boxer hits hard because his muscles are propelled from a state of ultimate relaxation to a condition of ultimate tensity. The energy produced by moving from one condition to the other produces the power of his punch. When I talk about being relaxed on the job, I am not talking about sleeping on the job. There are already too many people who are relaxed in this way. I am talking about reducing nervous tension, which causes or contributes to a great many of modern man's maladies. It plays a major part in heart ailments, ulcers, high blood pressure, and many many other malfunctions of the body. Self-hypnosis will help you relax physically.

Mentally, you will increase your powers of concentration and memory. Creative powers you never thought existed within you will begin to enrich your life. New horizons of intellectual endeavor will be opened to you.

Spiritually, self-hypnosis will make you a better disciple of your particular faith. I don't believe self-hypnosis is prayer, but I do believe that when you are fully engaged in spiritual prayer you are in a state of self-hypnosis. Self-hypnosis will help you concentrate your mind more completely on your God. The use of self-hypnosis will not conflict with the teachings of any of the major faiths.

Self-hypnosis can and will enrich every area of your life.

HIGHLIGHTS TO REMEMBER FROM THIS CHAPTER:

1. Self-hypnosis is the one tool that will enable you to realize your full potential in life.
2. Men fear hypnosis because they don't understand it.
3. Self-hypnosis is a God-given power which resides in everyone.
4. Successful men are not possessed by a power, but possess and control the power within them.
5. All the great men of the past, even though they knew nothing about hypnosis, were self-hypnotized men.
6. More is demanded of man's mental powers today than ever before. Self-hypnosis is the one tool that can meet this need.
7. Self-hypnosis can revive the 92 per cent of unused mind power in the average individual.
8. Anyone with a normal mind and a desire to learn self-hypnosis can succeed.
9. The only proof of really effective hypnosis is the post-hypnotic response.
10. Some people will have to hypnotize themselves a number of times before they get the post-hypnotic response they desire. It is recommended that you allow six weeks to obtain your goal.
11. Self-hypnosis can make a positive contribution to every phase of your life; physically, mentally, and spiritually.

2

WHAT IS SELF-HYPNOSIS
AND HOW DOES IT WORK?

"I THINK IT'S ALL A fake." I don't think there is any such thing as hypnosis." These are remarks I overheard as I left an auditorium where a stage hypnotist had just performed.

It seems people fall into three categories in regard to hypnosis. Some express the viewpoint just mentioned: They don't believe there is any such thing as hypnosis. Others are terribly afraid of it. To them it is the most dangerous, menacing thing in the world. The last group is greatly in favor of hypnosis. Some, in their zeal for hypnosis, go to extremes, but the majority are using it for the beneficial good of mankind.

To help us better understand hypnosis, let's do some of the unlearning we talked about in the last chapter. Let us consider some of the most common misconceptions.

HYPNOSIS IS NOT SLEEP

The error entertained by more people than any other is that hypnosis is sleep. Nothing could be further from the truth. It is easy to understand, however, why you might believe this. First, it is a popular misconception. Almost everyone believes hypnosis is sleep. Secondly, when you see someone being hypnotized he ultimately closes his eyes.

Dr. James Braid, a famous nineteenth century English physician, was at first deceived into thinking hypnosis, then known as Mesmerism, was sleep. He went to see a stage performer use hypnosis, with the intention of proving the man a fake and a fraud. After witnessing the man's abilities, he became firmly convinced there was something real about Mesmerism. Dr. Braid started to experiment on his own. His first subjects were his wife and servants. From his first observances, Braid came to the conclusion that Mesmerism was sleep. He took, therefore, the Greek word "hypno," which means sleep, and Mesmerism was changed to hypnosis. A little later he realized his mistake and tried to change the designation from hypnosis to mono-ideism, but he was never successful. Many men since that time have tried to change the designation 'hypnosis,' but none has ever been able to effect a change.

Hypnosis is in no way related to sleep. *A hypnotized individual is very conscious and very aware.* I can hypnotize people without having them close their eyes, and without talking about sleep or relaxation or using any of the other common hypnotic terminology. Time and time again I have demonstrated this, both in the privacy of my office and before both large and small groups. Out of a group of fifty or more, it is easy to find a number of people who will hallucinate all five of the physical senses. There are a number of authorities who make a distinction between this and hypnosis by calling this technique "waking suggestion," but to me, this distinction is strictly academic. Hypnosis is hypnosis, and whether the eyes are open or shut makes no difference.

One of my favorite demonstrations before sales groups is to actually sell one of the salesmen a piece of gold bullion which is nothing but a piece of air. I usually sell the air for a thousand dollars with twenty-five, fifty, or a hundred dollars down. These people are strangers. No eye closure, no talk of sleep or relaxation is involved. The fact that these individuals hallucinate visually indicates they are in the deepest stages of hypnosis. This should prove to you that hypnosis is not sleep. It also points out the fact that you do not become unconscious when you are hypnotized.

INTELLIGENT PEOPLE ARE EASIER TO HYPNOTIZE

Some of you are perhaps saying to yourself, "Well, these are ignorant, gullible people, but I am too intelligent for something like that to happen to me." This idea brings us to the second popular misconception in regard to hypnosis: only the stupid and gullible can be hypnotized. The reverse is true. *An intelligent person is easier to hypnotize.* The intelligent, informed person doesn't have the fears an ignorant person has. This doesn't mean all intelligent people are easily hypnotized, but it does mean that intelligence is in your favor. Many say that only a complete moron can not be hypnotized.

There is a distinct difference between being gullible and being suggestible. A gullible person is usually an ignorant individual who will believe anything, no matter how unrealistic it might be. A suggestible person, and we are all suggestible, is one who believes something if it can be presented to him in a realistic, convincing manner. The men to whom I sell the gold bullion are usually the top salesmen in their firms. Most of them have college degrees and are highly intelligent.

CAN HYPNOSIS OPERATE AGAINST MORAL WILL?

Another worry about hypnosis: "Will I do something against my moral will?" This has nothing to do with self-hypnosis, because when you hypnotize yourself you are giving yourself suggestions.

However, it is good that you be informed about this point. It is very remotely possible, but certainly not very probable, that one would violate his moral will. To get someone to go against his moral will the hypnotist would have to have daily access to the person and use brain washing techniques and subterfuge over a long period of time. The possibility of this is very, very slim. I know of only one crime committed as a result of hypnotic influence, and in that incident both the hypnotist and his subject were already criminals. There certainly wasn't any abridgement of the moral will.

We are safe in assuming that a hypnotized individual will not violate his moral will. It has been my personal experience that a person will not violate his will morally or otherwise. On occasions I have asked people to do simple, innocuous things, but they refused. When asked why, they would give a reason the average person would never dream of. I once asked a musician, who was in deep hypnosis, to sing a song. He flatly refused! No matter how I worded the suggestion he would not oblige me. After he awakened, I asked him why he wouldn't sing. He said the only thing he could think of was that he belonged to the union and was supposed to be paid for singing.

Many of you have seen stage hypnotists perform and have witnessed people doing very silly things—things they would not ordinarily do. This might seem to negate what we have said about people not violating their moral will. But it really doesn't. When an individual volunteers to be a subject in a theatre or night club where a hypnotist is performing, he automatically gives his consent to be tricked, fooled, and laughed at. There is no violation of the moral will.

ARE THERE POSSIBLE BAD EFFECTS ON THE WILL OR BRAIN?

Still another misconception about hypnosis is that hypnosis will weaken the will and perhaps do damage to the brain. This is not true. Hypnosis itself—the state of hypnosis—does no harm whatsoever. In fact, the relaxation does you a tremendous amount of good. Self-hypnosis, instead of weakening the will, strengthens it. In learning self-hypnosis you learn how to concentrate. You learn how to control your thoughts and your imagination. All of these factors are involved in strengthening, not weakening, the power of your will.

EXPLODING THE MYTH OF DANGER IN HYPNOTISM

Quite often you hear or read of the dangers of hypnosis. Now, I want to ask you a question, and I want you to give it some thought. Have you ever heard anyone explain what these dangers are? Have you known anyone who ever pinpointed or specified these dangers? I believe most of you will have to say, "no." An emotional subject, such as hypnotism, will bring out crackpots on both sides of the fence—the "joiner" and the "againster." You hear all kinds of weird stories, but when you get down to the facts you find them to be either unfounded or greatly exaggerated. It has been estimated that between five to twenty million Americans have been hypnotized in the past decade. Literally thousands have been taught self-hypnosis. Yet, as far as I know, no one has been harmed as a direct result of hypnosis or self-hypnosis.

Actually, the greatest danger involved in the use of hypnosis is to the hypnotist, not to the subject. Most states have no laws regulating the use of hypnosis, and anyone using it leaves himself wide open to all kinds of legal action. If a physician uses hypnosis on a patient who later gets cancer, the patient's spouse immediately blames hypnosis for causing the cancer. Litigations, grief, and expense are the result.

If you were to ask me the direct question, "Is hypnosis dangerous?" I would answer with another question: "Is it dangerous to be awake or asleep?" You say, "What does that have to do with it?" Everything! The hypnotic state is just as normal and natural as being awake or being asleep.

HYPNOTISM A WAY OF LIFE

If you think about it for a moment, you will find that most of the things you do every day are done more on a subconscious than on a conscious level. When you drive you aren't conscious or aware of what you are doing. You don't say to yourself, "Turn the corner, push on the brakes . . ." If you were to do this you would be a poor driver indeed. When you first learned to drive you drove this way, but now you drive more on the subconscious level. Notice, not on the sleep level, but on the subconscious level.

Typing is another example. A good typist isn't aware of where her fingers are moving. Her subconscious is directing them.

Anything you do well is done on a hypnotic basis—dancing, reading, any athletic skill. . . .

As I stated at the beginning of the book, you have been hypnotized every day of your life. With this in mind, we can now answer your question, "Is hypnosis dangerous?" Whether hypnosis is dangerous or not would depend on the circumstances. It isn't dangerous to be in the company of good friends while awake, but it is dangerous to be in the presence of criminals and charlatans. It isn't dangerous to be asleep in your own bed, but it is dangerous to be asleep in a skid-row alley. The same principles apply to the hypnotic state. If you allow yourself to be hypnotized at a party by someone who has read a two-dollar book on hypnosis, you might suffer some temporary discomfort, but if you allow yourself to be hypnotized by a trained, competent person you would no doubt receive some gratifying results.

THE TRUE CONCEPT

Now that we have dealt with some of the more prevalent misconceptions about hypnosis, let us tell you the truth about hypnosis and self-hypnosis. The two, hypnosis and self-hypnosis, are one and the same. The only difference is that in hetero-hypnosis the hypnotist guides your thoughts; whereas in self-hypnosis you guide your own thoughts. Remember—all hypnosis is self-hypnosis. On the positive suggestion level, whatever a hypnotist can do for you, you can do for yourself if you are trained in self-hypnosis. Notice also that I said on the "positive suggestion level." This would not apply to those who have a severe emotional or mental difficulty. These individuals should seek help from a competent psychotherapist before learning self-hypnosis.

Let me now explain what I mean when I say that hypnosis is a normal, natural state, and you have been hypnotized every day of your life. Have you ever read a book, watched a television program, or been so engrossed in anything that when someone called you, you didn't pay any attention to them or you didn't hear them? Well, that is hypnosis. Any time your mind is exclusively, or almost exclusively, on one thing, you are hypnotized.

Hypnosis is defined as being "an altered state of consciousness." It is also defined as being a state of "hypersuggestibility." When you are hypnotized you are conscious, but your consciousness is limited primarily to the suggestions you are receiving. There are degrees of consciousness. For instance, if I were to ask right now if you are conscious, you would say, "Well, of course I am." And it is true; you must be conscious if you are reading this book. Yet, the consciousness you are experiencing now is different, in degree, from the consciousness you felt this morning when you first got out of bed. I should qualify this by saying that this is true if you are like me in this respect. It takes me about two hours to get completely awake. Yet when I first get up, I'm conscious, but not as conscious as at other times. If you were walking across a street and an automobile started toward you at a high rate of speed, you would really become conscious. Your brain, nervous system, glands, heart, and muscles would all spring into full action to save you from possible death or injury. From these few examples, you can see there are different degrees of consciousness. You are more conscious at one time than you are at another time.

When you are in hypnosis your attention span (consciousness) is narrowed to the thought or idea being given you at that moment. You are experiencing consciousness in one of its highest forms. In a normal state of consciousness, you are aware of many things: objects, people, noises, odors, and everything about you. Whereas, in hypnosis you are totally aware of one thing. You might hear other noises, etc., but they mean little or nothing to you. Your mind is riveted to one thing—the thought you are giving yourself. This is self-hypnosis.

THE STATE OF HYPERSUGGESTIBILITY

When you are in hypnosis you are in a state of hypersuggestibility. "Hyper" means increased. You are susceptible to suggestions at all times. Have you ever been in a crowd when someone begins to cough? It isn't long before a number of people begin to cough. Have you ever watched a T.V. commercial advertising a delicious looking food? You got hungry, didn't you? Don't ever fool yourself by believing you aren't suggestible. If you do, you will be a bright prospect for the next con-artist that comes to your town.

We are suggestible at all times, but more so when we are in hypnosis. The conscious mind possesses what we will call the "critical faculty," and when we are hypnotized this critical faculty is relaxed. The critical faculty is our power of evaluation and discernment. When it is relaxed suggestions go directly into the subconscious. The subconscious accepts these suggestions literally. If you suggest that your hands will feel as heavy as two chunks of lead, they begin to feel as heavy as two chunks of lead. If you were in a normal state of consciousness with your critical faculty fully operative, this wouldn't work. The conscious mind would evaluate and say, "My hands aren't two chunks of lead, and they don't feel heavy." When it is relaxed the suggestion becomes a reality.

The subconscious doesn't possess a "critical faculty." Many authorities believe the subconscious has a "feedback mechanism"

—what you feed into the subconscious is fed back into your conscious life. If you are told all of your life, "You are no good; you are trash," and you accept these thoughts and feed them into the subconscious, you will have a terrific inferiority complex. If the idea that you are a good, nice individual with a potential in life is given to you by your neighbors, friends, and relatives, and you accept this idea and feed it into your subconscious, the subconscious will feed it back into your life and you will be a confident person.

One important thing should be pointed out at this time. What someone says or thinks about you doesn't affect your subconscious unless you accept their suggestions. Nothing gets into the subconscious unless it comes through the conscious mind. The young man who has been told that he is no good will not be affected by these attitudes unless he accepts them as facts. If he is able to "control" his stream of thought, he can actually grow in self-confidence. Nothing anyone says to you, no matter how bad or horrible it may be, can hurt you, unless you accept what they say. You are the only one who can hurt yourself, and you do this by believing and accepting unpleasant things which are said to or about you. Cast them aside. Forget them. Don't keep re-hashing them in your mind so that it will sink into the subconscious and be there to haunt you. Forget it, period.

THE SOURCE OF DIFFICULTIES
AND FAILURES IN LIFE

Most of the difficulties and failures in your life are due to the fact that your subconscious is a reservoir of a vast amount of misinformation. Your subconscious needs to be re-educated and reprogramed. Dr. Maxwell Maltz in his book, *Psycho-Cybernetics* (published by Prentice-Hall, Inc., Englewood Cliffs, N.J.) reveals the fact that most of us need to be dehypnotized. This is why it is almost impossible for you to gain self-confidence or self-improvement in any area of your life without using the dynamics of hypnosis or self-hypnosis. The subconscious must be reached and be convinced with new and forceful suggestions if you are to achieve what you desire in your life.

A young woman came to my office with a very serious problem. For three months she had been unable to sleep for more than a few moments at a time. She had seen a number of doctors, but no one could bring her relief. I hypnotized her and discovered she had been to see a fortune-teller at the exact time her insomnia started. The fortune-teller told her she was going to die in the near future. This thought so frightened her that she repressed it deeply in her subconscious and consciously forgot about it. She couldn't sleep because she was afraid. As long as she was awake she knew she was alive, but to sleep might mean death. When she became aware of these things, and had her thinking re-educated, she slept like a baby.

As a child your mind is filled with many fantasies: Santa Claus, the good fairies, etc. Later in your teens and early twenties you enter the idealistic period of life. It is at this time when you are fed many other fantasies—fantasies of a different type, I grant you, but nonetheless, fantasies. It is not my intention to cast disparagement on idealism or the idealistic age. But I believe those of you who have passed through this period of life know what I mean when I say we are filled with many fantasies at that time. It was at this period in my life when I felt I could change and save the world, but I have long since learned differently. This doesn't mean that I have become a pessimist, but I have become more realistic.

If used effectively, self-hypnosis can be a powerful tool in your life to effect change where change is necessary, and to re-educate the mind to a new, realistic, and sound way of thinking.

HIGHLIGHTS TO REMEMBER FROM THIS CHAPTER:

1. Hypnosis is not sleep.
2. All the phenomena of hypnosis can be produced in the so-called "waking state."
3. An intelligent individual is easier to hypnotize than a not-so-intelligent person.
4. You will not violate your moral beliefs or lose your will while under hypnosis.
5. Hypnosis does not weaken the mind or will.
6. Hypnosis is a normal, natural state.
7. Most of your daily functions are accomplished on a subconscious level.
8. All hypnosis is self-hypnosis.
9. Hypnosis is "an altered state of consciousness."

10. Hypnosis is a state of hypersuggestibility.
11. The conscious mind possesses a "critical faculty."
12. The subconscious possesses a feedback mechanism.
13. Most people need to be dehypnotized.
14. Self-hypnosis is the most effective way to effect change in your life.

3

YOU ARE WHAT YOU BELIEVE SUBCONSCIOUSLY

THE NATURE OF HYPNOSIS

A THEORY WHICH EXPLAINS HYPNOSIS clearly is one set forth by Dr. William S. Kroger, M.D., in his *Clinical & Experimental Hypnosis* published by J. B. Lippincott Company. Dr. Kroger believes that hypnosis is a "conviction phenomenon."

Simply stated, "conviction phenomenon" means that if you believe something strongly enough it becomes real to you. In hypnosis your subconscious, which accepts data uncritically, is convinced of certain facts. When your subconscious is convinced, these things become real to you.

MENTAL CONVICTION UNDER HYPNOSIS

While under deep hypnosis an individual can allow himself to be convinced. The hypnotist tells him that a thin sheet of paper weighs a thousand pounds. Even though he struggles with all his strength, the hypnotized subject is unable to lift the sheet of paper. Ordinarily he would be able to lift it with no effort whatsoever. Why can't he lift it now? The answer is simple: He has allowed himself to be convinced the paper is too heavy. Notice, he isn't told he is too weak to lift it, but that the paper is too heavy for him to lift.

Another example of a different nature is producing a blister or rash by hypnotic suggestion. After a subject has been put into deep hypnosis, the hypnotist tells him he is going to be touched with a hot poker and his skin will blister. The hypnotist proceeds to touch him, not with a hot poker, but with a pencil or his finger or nothing at all, and a blister forms on the subject's flesh.

It is common knowledge among those who work with hypnosis that it is possible to produce a rash with suggestion. The procedure for this is much the same as that for producing a blister. In this case, however, it is usually necessary to find someone who is allergic to something which causes a rash. While under hypnosis the person is told that the item to which he is allergic is being rubbed against his skin, and shortly a rash appears. Nothing, of course, is rubbed against his skin—only words are used.

The important factor to be noted here is that the subconscious is so powerful that when it is convinced it can produce a physiological change in the body.

A man in a deep hypnotic trance is told he is going to jump from a height of ten feet. Actually, he will be jumping six inches. But, although he will jump only six inches physically, physiologically he will jump ten feet. The reason is: he is convinced he is jumping ten feet. Time distortion, space distortion, and many other factors play a part in this phenomenon.

Many times I have hypnotized people and told them they were eating a delicious steak dinner. They chew and swallow the food. Their digestive systems go to work. Quite often they are just as satisfied with the imaginary meal as they would be with a real meal.

We could go on and on citing examples for you, but I believe these are sufficient to prove the importance of "belief" in hypnosis. When your subconscious believes something, it affects every phase of your existence. It is capable of producing the most profound psychological, physiological, and physical reactions in your life. You have heard that a man is what he believes. I will go a step further and state that a man is what he believes subconsciously. There are many things in which you glibly say you believe, but you believe them on a conscious, verbal level, not subconsciously. Things which you believe consciously have no effect on your life or your behavior. But what you believe or are convinced of on a subconscious level has a tremendous effect on your life and behavior.

THE ENIGMA OF CONSCIOUS AND SUBCONSCIOUS MOTIVATION

Quite often you will not admit to your conscious mind what you believe subconsciously, usually because you don't want to go against social mores and customs. Yet, the beliefs that motivate most people are beliefs they seldom if ever express verbally, and the things they say they believe consciously don't motivate them.

Subconscious beliefs are the result of many factors. The repetition of certain ideas by parents, relatives, schoolteachers and friends can influence them. They are also caused by inference, for the aforementioned individuals might have said one thing, but demonstrated something entirely different with their lives. Subconscious beliefs can be the result of one or more traumatic experiences. They are the result of everything we have read, heard, or experienced which has reached the subconscious.

At this point, you might be saying to yourself, "What do I believe subconsciously?" "How can I know what I believe subconsciously?" There is only one way to answer these questions: Subconscious belief affects conscious behaviour. The subconscious feeds back into our lives what it has uncritically accepted from the conscious mind. You might consciously tell yourself that you have self-confidence, that you are not afraid to talk to people. But the fact is you don't talk to people. Many times you lose a potential friend or contact because you are hesitant to take the initiative and speak up. Your actions demonstrate that your subconscious is convinced you are inferior in these areas. The scope of this truth is unlimited. Men and women are failures, men and women are slaves to habit, men and women are emotional cripples, not because they consciously want to be, but because their subconscious has been convinced they have to be!

THE SUBCONSCIOUS CAN BE REACHED BY HYPNOSIS

This might sound hopeless, but it really isn't. The subconscious can be reached by hypnosis and self-hypnosis. It can not only be reached, but it can be re-educated and convinced in the correct way.

A man whose subconscious has been convinced of a certain

fact can try to change this thing in his life on a conscious level from now until the day he dies, but he will never be completely successful.

Let us go back to the man who lacks self-confidence. He can take public speaking courses and self-confidence courses; he can force himself to speak to people and to be a mixer, but he will never really achieve self-confidence by any of these methods. The only way he can obtain self-confidence is by re-educating the subconscious. He must, literally, erase his old subconscious beliefs and replace them with new positive beliefs.

FAILURE AS A MATTER OF CONVICTION

Men are not failures because it is necessary that they be failures. God doesn't want them to be failures. Their employers don't want them to be failures. When a man is making money for himself, he is making money for his employer. Men fail because their subconscious has been convinced they must fail.

I recently worked with a young sales executive who was employed by a large engineering firm. This young man had everything imaginable in his favor to make him a resounding success. He possessed a good family background. He did well in college. His personality was gregarious and warm. His appearance was pleasing, and he was an excellent dresser. These are all surface qualities that help to make one successful. Yet when he came to me, he was on the brink of his third failure. He had worked for two firms previous to this one, and both times it was the same story. He would start out like a dynamo. No one in the office could keep up with him or match his sales record. Other salesmen envied and hated him. His superiors praised and encouraged him.

Then slowly, but surely, his sales would start to decline. He would hit a few "dry runs" and become discouraged. He just couldn't force himself to continue. No matter what he tried, nothing could arouse his enthusiasm or hope. Eventually he would give up, blaming all his troubles on the company and the product. True, he would get another job, but the same thing would occur again. Each time this happened he lost more of his self-esteem. When he was honest with himself, he knew he was a quitter. He was intelligent enough to know something was wrong, and he could discern the pattern which was set in his life—he always lost enthusiasm and quit after a couple of rejections.

As he talked with me, he would state that he knew when men rejected his product they were not rejecting him. He knew that every salesman has slow periods. He knew he shouldn't get discouraged and quit. But all of this conscious knowledge did not help him because he didn't believe any of it subconsciously.

By talking with him, and through the use of hypnosis, I found a number of factors which created the failure proneness in his life. As a child his life had been filled with more than the usual number of emotional disappointments. He always had the best money could buy, but he never felt loved or accepted by his father. His father was a highly successful, self-made man, and he was constantly putting his son to the test. As long as he met his father's demands he was wonderful, but when he failed there was always a long period of rejection. The father would often castigate him and tell him that he just didn't have the guts and backbone to stay with anything. This was repeated so often by his father that the subconscious was thoroughly convinced this was a fact. His mother was a "milktoast" woman, whose supersensitivity rubbed off on him.

When he became aware of these and other factors and learned a self-hypnosis technique, he quickly overcame this barrier to success. I taught him how to convince himself subconsciously that he could succeed, and that he could stay with any situation, no matter how difficult, and win.

Many of you are not as successful as you would like to be. The reason for your lack of success is the same as this young man's. You have allowed yourself to be convinced subconsciously that you can succeed only so far and then you have to stop. You possess a success barrier which will not allow you to succeed beyond a certain point.

THE CAUSE OF FAILURE NEED NOT ALWAYS BE KNOWN

It is not always necessary that you become aware of the cause of your failure. I have worked with a number of people who have overcome their difficulties by using positive suggestions while under self-induced hypnosis. The mind seems to be like a tape recorder. It is possible to erase old, negative thoughts and patterns with new, positive thoughts and patterns. Here is the technique I teach. You must determine what your actual conduct or habit pattern is—not what you think and believe consciously, but what you actually do. The reason for this, as we have already stated, is that *you do what the subconscious believes.* After you have done this, write out a suggestion to use with your self-hypnosis. Amazing results can be achieved with this simple technique. Those who have severe problems should, of course, seek professional help.

A CASE HISTORY SUMMARY OF FAILURE
AND SUCCESS

I know another man who is just the opposite of the man we have been discussing. The third grade was the extent of his formal education. He is from a very poor, uneducated family. He is similar to the other man in that he has a nice appearance and a very outstanding personality. This gentleman, despite his lack of formal education and family background, is highly successful. If you talked with him you would soon know the reason. His parents instilled within him the idea that someday he would be a great and successful man. He had to quit school after the third grade to help support the family. However, that didn't stop him. He read everything he could beg, buy, or borrow. He made every job he had an enterprise and gradually became very outstanding in his field. Dad and Mom were always proud of his every achievement and constantly convinced him of his inevitable greatness.

The difference between the two men: One had been convinced subconsciously he would ultimately fail because he couldn't stick to anything—the other was convinced subconsciously that no matter what he did he would succeed.

There are men who become successful without the right kind of encouragement from their parents. These men usually identify themselves with men who are successful and create a burning desire to attain this success. They literally hypnotize themselves into becoming men of renown.

Not only can people be convinced subconsciously concerning

their success or failure, but they can also be convinced subconsciously whether they will be happy or unhappy. There are individuals who have everything a human could want: loving mate, children, social position and material comforts, yet they find some way to become unhappy. They literally seek out and find something that will make them unhappy. Consciously, they tell you they know they should be happy and want to be happy, but nothing seems to satisfy them. The reason is, of course, that subconsciously they have been convinced they cannot be happy.

CASE HISTORY OF A PERSON WHO "WAS AFRAID TO BE HAPPY"

Some years ago, I knew a lady who said she couldn't find peace and happiness in life. This particular lady was a Christian whose religious beliefs were similar to mine. While talking with her one day, she made the remark that she was "afraid" to be happy. I hypnotized her and used the word "afraid" as a trigger to uncover why she was afraid to be happy. She revealed that in her early years her parents were always apprehensive if things were going well. They convinced her that difficult times were around the corner. Don't enjoy good times because they don't last. Don't trust anyone or anything. Always be on the defensive. She had been hypnotized into believing it was impossible for her to be happy. Happiness was unobtainable as far as she was concerned.

This woman had a devoted husband and two lovely children. Their finances were more than adequate to meet their needs and supply them with a few pleasures. She declared consciously her faith in the all-sufficient grace of God. The fact was, however, she believed something far different in her subconscious, and this was the motivating factor in her life. With the use of hypnosis and self-hypnosis she re-educated her subconscious into believing it was God's will for her to be happy and to have the inner peace which Christ had promised her.

The other side of this coin is the individual who has very little of this world's goods and who is what we might call a "nobody," but who is extremely happy. I am sure every reader knows someone who would fit this description. This doesn't mean people have to be poor in order to be happy. There are many poor people who are very unhappy, and I am sure there are wealthy people who are happy.

The fact of the matter is this: Outward circumstances have little to do with being happy or unhappy. It is the inner attitude, the belief of the subconscious, which is the determining factor. Some people, because of early conditioning, believe subconsciously they can't be happy unless they move in certain circles, live in particular neighbourhoods, or make so much money per year. Other people are convinced subconsciously that wealth is sinful and brings troubles and heartaches.

It is imperative that you re-educate your subconscious to believe you can be happy in any and all circumstances.

THE ORIGIN OF PSYCHOSOMATIC DISEASE

It is estimated by medical authorities that approximately seventy-five per cent of all sick people are afflicted with psychosomatic diseases. This simply means the origin of their disease is more emotional than it is physical. It is possible for a person to become blind, deaf, or paralyzed even though there is nothing wrong with their eyes, ears, or limbs. These people are not faking. Their blindness, deafness, or paralysis is real. These particular maladies are caused by a trauma or shock. A number of servicemen suffered in this manner during the First and Second World Wars. It was found that hypnosis was one of the best ways to treat these conditions. This was one of the main contributing factors in bringing about the resurgence of medical hypnosis.

When a trauma is effected in an individual the subconscious is convinced that it is better not to see or hear, etc. Life is too horrible to look upon or listen to. This might seem like an oversimplification to some, but I don't really think it is because, when the affected individual is convinced under hypnosis that "all is well; the war is over; it is alright for you to see once again," his sight usually returns. Reliving the experience while under hypnosis is part of the usual treatment, but, to me, this is also a part of the reconvincing of the subconscious.

There are many sick people who were not shocked into their illnesses. By one means or another, such a person's subconscious has been convinced that he is sick. Sometimes the subconscious is led to believe that he is guilty and has a need to be punished. The subconscious then proceeds to devise an illness which will compensate for the guilt. Quite often the subconscious is impressed with the fact that the best way to get attention is by being sick.

Identification is another way by which the subconscious is persuaded to produce illness. An individual identifies himself with a relative who has an illness or affliction. He is told by his mother he will probably have the same disease, and this is so impressed on his mind that eventually the disease does become a reality. There are many other ways the subconscious may be convinced that the organism has a need of being sick. The paramount fact to remember is that, whether it be a case of illness, success or failure, happiness or unhappiness, when the subconscious is convinced of a matter it becomes a reality in your life.

SUBCONSCIOUS BELIEF AS A CAUSE OF DEATH

Subconscious belief is so powerful it can actually cause death. A case in point is that of the voodoo worshippers. From the time of infancy, they are taught that if someone pierces a voodoo doll which represents them, they will die. The fact is people actually die when this takes place. Now, why do they die? Is it because the person with the doll has a mystical power or that the doll itself can implement death? No, the answer is simply this: Because of a lifetime of conditioning, the subconscious is convinced that death will come if the voodoo hex is placed upon the individual. When the doll is pierced it causes such a shock death occurs.

Case History: Did a "Broken" Heart Cause Her Death?

There are other cases in our own modern society where people begin to age prematurely and die because of suggestion. Their subconscious becomes convinced they are going to die, and they die. Fantastic, but nonetheless true! I am reminded of a situation concerning a woman in her late thirties who had never married but had gone with one man for fifteen years. They were never formally engaged, but everyone thought someday they would be married. Suddenly, he announced he was going to marry another woman. She had no idea that he was interested in anyone else. For fifteen years they had done everything together. All of her hopes for the future were based on this man. When he broke the news to her about his marriage she fell apart emotionally for a few days. Then it seemed she got hold of herself. She came out of seclusion, went back to work, and resumed her normal routine. In a matter of weeks, however, she started to age! Her skin started to wrinkle. She lost weight and appeared drawn! Her hair turned gray! She became feeble!

The best medical help was sought for her. She was hospitalized and examinations were made, but nothing could be found that would account for her condition. In less than a year, she was dead. She died because her subconscious was convinced that life wasn't worth living without her lover. *It could be said she died of a broken heart, but the truth is she died because of a "convinced subconscious."*

A TURNING POINT OF LIFE OR DEATH

Subconscious belief can also cause people to live when death seems certain. I have witnessed this phenomenon a number of times. Before I knew anything about hypnosis, I am sure I hypnotized people on the critical list into living. Every clergyman and doctor has had the same experience. The individual who is critically ill comes to a point where life or death depends on whether he believes he will live or die. If he is convinced subconsciously he can live, he lives! If he believes he can't live or face further suffering, he dies.

A striking example of this happened in the life of a close friend. When he was twelve he had a severe case of pneumonia and for several days hovered between life and death. This was before the discovery of all the wonderful modern drugs. One night, when he was very critical, he heard the physician tell his mother that he was going to give a new medication and expected him to be much better and on the road to recovery by morning. This proved to be true: when he awakened he felt better than he had for days. He was definitely past the critical stage. Later it was learned that the nurse gave him the wrong medication. By mistake, she gave him the same medication he had been taking all along. My friend thinks he was healed because he thoroughly believed what the physician said about the new drug. It would make him well over-night.

The classical placebo or sugar pill is another example. A pa-tient comes to the doctor with a complaint and the doctor gives him a pill which contains nothing of a medicinal nature. He takes the pill and feels much better.

AN EXPLANATION OF RELIGIOUS HEALING: A PERFECT EXAMPLE OF SELF-HYPNOTISM

The "conviction phenomena" is also the answer that explains all religious healings. The afflicted individual is convinced that if he receives the prayers and blessings of a particular gifted man, or if certain people will pray for him, or if he can go to a special, holy shrine, he will be healed. Many times this is exactly what happens. I do not deny the power of God to heal. God can choose any instrument he desires to effect healing. I merely say this is a scientific explanation of his miraculous power. I believe all heal-ing comes from God whether it be by medicine, surgery, prayer, or suggestion.

Subconscious belief is the most powerful factor in your life. It determines all of your behavior patterns. It determines what you are and what you are going to be. In the following chapters, we are going to show you practical methods by which you can effectively reach the subconscious and change and govern what you believe.

HIGHLIGHTS TO REMEMBER FROM THIS CHAPTER:

1. Hypnosis is a "conviction phenomenon." In its ramifications it can explain religious healing.
2. When the subconscious becomes convinced of a fact, whether it be true or false, it becomes a reality in your life.
3. The subconscious is capable of affecting you physically and psychologically.
4. You are what you believe subconsciously. What the subcon-scious believes feeds back into your conscious life and de-termines your behavior patterns.
5. You can determine what you believe subconsciously by ana-lyzing your conscious behavior.
6. What you believe subconsciously can determine whether you

will be unsuccessful or successful, happy or unhappy, healthy or sick, alive or dead.

7. Hypnosis is the most effective way to reach and re-educate the subconscious.

4

PRELIMINARY STEPS
IN SELF-HYPNOSIS

WHEN AN INDIVIDUAL STARTS TO learn how to play the piano, he doesn't start with Mozart or Chopin. He begins by learning to play the scales. Later he learns to play actual musical compositions. The young man who goes out to make the football team doesn't begin to play football immediately. First, he runs and runs, then he performs all kinds of exercises. Finally, after about six weeks, the coach lets him play a little football.

THE BASIS OF A PROGRAM

The same thing is true in regard to achieving self-hypnosis. You must begin at the beginning. The scales must be learned, exercises have to be performed. The mind is similar to the body in that it has to be conditioned and trained. There is no easy way to become proficient at self-hypnosis. It is true that the average person can learn self-hypnosis in a relatively short period of time. But if you want to be effective with self-hypnosis, you must apply yourself diligently.

Now, I don't want to frighten you into thinking this is something which is going to involve more time than you have available. Actually, the time needed is only fifteen minutes a day. At first, you will need to practice daily until you feel you have achieved real self-hypnosis. After this, it will be necessary to practice only once or twice a week to stay in good condition. Of course, when you are working on a particular improvement it will be necessary to use self-hypnosis on a daily basis. I am stressing these things so you won't think you can achieve self-hypnosis by some magical formula.

The best and quickest way to learn self-hypnosis is to first be hypnotized by a hypnotist. While under hypnosis, have him tell you that in the future you will be able to effectively hypnotize yourself. Usually six to ten sessions with a hypnotist are necessary for you to learn self-hypnosis. I teach a group course in self-hypnosis which meets once a week for eight weeks. Each class session lasts for at least two hours. The first hour is devoted to lectures dealing with self-hypnosis, and the second hour is devoted to group hypnosis. Eighty-five per cent of the people who take my course are able to hypnotize themselves by the time the course is completed. The remaining fifteen per cent learn to relax and are able to use the rules of suggestion we teach them to their advantage.

FINDING A QUALIFIED HYPNOTIST

Finding a qualified hypnotist is not always the easiest thing to do. Here are some guide lines you can follow in selecting a man who uses hypnosis. If possible, secure the services of a professional man who is engaged in either the healing or teaching arts. Choose a man who has a public responsibility. Physicians, psychologists, dentists, ministers, teachers, or lawyers are all responsible to some governing body. Judge the hypnotist on the basis of his training and experience in the field of hypnosis. A physician might be a good bone surgeon, but know very little about hypnosis. A clergyman might know a lot about theology, but he might be a poor hypnotist. The American Institute of Hypnosis will refer you to a professional man engaged in the practice of hypnosis; write to: The American Institute of Hypnosis, 8833 Sunset Boulevard, Los Angeles, California. If you can't find a professional man, contact the A.A.E.H., 10 Washington Ave., Irvington, New Jersey. They will gladly direct you to a qualified lay-hypnotist in your area.

Phonograph recordings and tape recordings dealing with self-hypnosis can also aid in your quest to attain self-hypnosis. There are a number of good recordings on the market today, which will be a help to the average individual.

BEGINNING A PROGRAM OF SELF-HELP FOR SELF-HYPNOSIS

Now that you know the quickest and easiest way to learn self-hypnosis, which, by the way, is also the most expensive, let me show you how to learn self-hypnosis on your own. *The biggest barrier in achieving self-hypnosis is not knowing how to recognize the state of hypnosis.* Therefore, I am going to repeat some very important facts for your guidance.

1. Hypnosis is a normal, natural state.
2. You do not fall asleep or become unconscious.
3. Hypnosis is a narrowing of the attention span to primarily one thing.
4. It is an altered state of consciousness.
5. It is a state of hypersuggestibility.
6. The only real proof of genuine, effective hypnosis or self-hypnosis is the post-hypnotic response.

Ninety-nine people out of a hundred that I hypnotize will tell me they don't believe they were in hypnosis. They will say, "But I heard everything you said, and I knew everything I was doing." People who go into very deep hypnosis respond with these words the same as those who do not go so deeply. It is, therefore, very important that you thoroughly understand the facts about self-hypnosis if you intend to accomplish it by yourself.

Beware of an overly analytical attitude: Another thing which will hinder you is an overly analytical attitude. *If you begin to analyze every move you make and doubt the effectiveness of what you are doing, it will be very difficult for you to go into self-hypnosis.* Instead of examining yourself, just relax and let go; the results will come. If you eat pie and ice cream as a steady diet, you get fat. If you exercise daily, you get strong. And thus, if you apply yourself to the things taught in this book, you will achieve self-hypnosis. Everyone who takes piano lessons doesn't become a concert pianist, but anyone who practices the piano long enough can learn to play well enough to give himself personal satisfaction. You may never be able to duplicate the feats of Houdini, but you will be able to improve different phases of your life if you will just practice.

The "prove it" attitude is another thing which will keep you from being effective with your self-hypnosis. There are always individuals who have an "I am from Missouri" attitude. They are so busy trying to decide whether they are or are not in hypnosis that they defeat their own efforts. A typical example of this is when a hypnotist, hypnotizing a subject for the first time, tells him that in a moment his eyes are going to close. The subject's eyes begin to close automatically, but he deliberately makes a definite effort to keep them open. He fights the suggestion of the hypnotist and the physical response of his eyes in order to prove something to himself. The thing he is trying to prove is something every good hypnotist already knows: you can't make a subject do anything he doesn't want to do. The only thing this type of individual does is to hinder and delay his hypnosis.

Pertaining to self-hypnosis, most people express the "prove it" attitude by constantly giving themselves tests. They give themselves a test, and if they don't pass it they feel as if they are making no progress. An old proverb says, "A watched pot never boils." This is very true of those who are "overly analytical" and possess a "prove it" attitude while learning to use self-hypnosis. I know a great deal about these two hindrances because I have experienced both of them. When I realized that these factors were obstacles to my self-hypnosis, I stopped doing them, and then I achieved real self-hypnosis. The thing which brought me success was just plain practicing the "scales" of self-hypnosis.

"Easy Does It" Will Do It For You: One other thing you should avoid is "trying too hard." This is rather difficult to explain because it sounds like a contradiction, but I will do my best. Whenever you become too anxious about anything, it makes you nervous and tense. And whenever you are in a state such as this, it is impossible to do your best. The tense driver is a poor driver. The tense student is a poor student. Tension is the greatest enemy of hypnosis. I have found that, when someone wants to be hypnotized so badly that he becomes overanxious and tense, I have to

spend a great deal of time calming and relaxing him before I can hypnotize him. This is especially true of people who expect miracles to be performed in one or two sessions of hypnosis.

ALLOW YOURSELF REASONABLE TIME

When you begin to learn self-hypnosis, give yourself time. Start as a beginner, don't expect miracles over night, and above all, forget yourself, let go and relax. Keep in mind at all times the thought that with consistent effort and practice you will achieve self-hypnosis. Don't allow yourself to be discouraged. I have yet to see the person who kept trying who didn't eventually learn how to hypnotize himself.

I worked with a close personal friend over three years. He had private instruction from me and used my self-hypnosis recordings so often that he literally wore them out. He also took my group course. He didn't merely take it once, but he took it three times. He received some gratifying results from the beginning, but he wasn't satisfied. One night while teaching the class, I mentioned the hindrances to hypnosis we have just considered. Then I proceeded to hypnotize the group and give suggestions concerning self-hypnosis. The next day my friend called and said, "Guess what?" and I said, "Guess what? what?" He answered, "I did it." "Did what?" was my reply. "I really hypnotized myself this morning."

Actually, he had been hypnotizing himself for three years, but he just had to prove it to himself by "passing a test." The important factor here, however, is that he did achieve self-hypnosis to his own satisfaction after three years of diligent effort. Most people will accomplish the same thing in much less time.

HOW TO SCHEDULE YOUR PRACTICE

To receive the best results you should practice at the same time and place every day. Most of you are extremely busy; therefore, you will have to make time. We take time to do what we want to do in life. Your wife might ask you to do something for her when you get home from work, but you tell her you have worked hard all day and are too tired. A little later in the evening a buddy calls and wants you to go bowling—you know the end of the story. Somehow or other, you get revived and go. If you want to get results in self-hypnosis, you must make time to practice.

When you are practicing self-hypnosis, make arrangements with someone to answer the door and the telephone. If it is something important the party will call again. After you have spent a couple of weeks in practice, the ringing of the phone won't bother you. You will hear it ring, but you can decide whether or not you wish to answer. It is possible to so condition yourself that you may answer the phone and when your conversation is finished immediately go back into hypnosis where you left off.

THE TOOLS WITH WHICH YOU WORK

The most vital things for you to remember when you begin the practice of self-hypnosis are the tools with which you are working. They are *suggestion and imagination*. The road which leads to hypnosis is *suggestion*, but the vehicle in which you travel is *imagination*. Anyone with a good imagination can easily achieve self-hypnosis. The secret is to find *in what way you are the most suggestible*. Remember, everyone is suggestible; therefore everyone can be hypnotized. It is just a matter of deciding how you respond best to suggestion. To determine this, try a few of these suggestion tests.

Test one. Place the ends of your thumb and middle finger together and push. At the same time look at them and imagine they are stuck together with glue. Also, imagine that adhesive tape has been wrapped tightly around your thumb nail and finger nail. Tell yourself, as you apply more pressure, that they are getting tighter and tighter. In fact, they are getting so tight they are completely stuck together and will not come apart. When you count to three, your finger and thumb will be stuck and will not come apart until you say the word, "NOW." The more you try to take them apart the tighter they will become. If you respond completely to this test, you will have no difficulty in learning to hypnotize yourself. If you do not respond too well you have no need to worry, because you will eventually find your area of suggestibility. You might be more effective if you do the test with your eyes closed.

Test two. While seated comfortably on a chair or lying on a bed, tell yourself the following:

"My eyes are becoming very relaxed. All of the muscles which control the movements of my eye-lids are becoming very loose and limp. They are becoming so loose and limp that in just a moment my eyes will close and be sealed shut. Once they are sealed I will be unable to open them until I say the word, 'NOW.' My eyes continue to relax. They are relaxing more and more. It feels as though lead weights have been attached to my lids pulling them down. My eyelids feel as though they are window shades and are being gently pulled down. My eyes continue to relax. In fact, they are getting so relaxed that when I count to three they close and seal shut. They will remain sealed until I say the word, 'NOW.' "

Most of you will respond to this test if you take your time and make good use of your imagination.

Test Three. Clasp your hands together and extend them in front of you. Close your eyes and imagine your hands are being fused together. Visualize them as being one solid block of wood. As you imagine these things gradually squeeze your hands tighter and tighter together. Say to yourself, "My hands are being completely fused together. They are becoming a solid block of wood. When I count three, I will be unable to take them apart until I say the word, 'NOW.' " Those who respond well to this test must have a strong imagination. When giving yourself this test, take your time and try, as much as possible, to see your hands as a solid block of wood.

Test Four. Seat yourself comfortably in a straight chair. Let your hands hang loosely at your sides. Close your eyes and imagine your hands are two lead weights. Say the following to yourself: "My hands are getting heavier and heavier. They feel as though they are lead weights. They are becoming heavier and heavier. They feel huge and ponderous. My hands feel lazy and tired. At this moment the most difficult thing for me to do would be to lift my hands because they are so heavy and lazy. When I count to three it will be impossible for me to lift my hand until I say the word, 'NOW.' "

Test Five. Once again, seat yourself comfortably in a straight chair. Place your feet flat on the floor. Let one of your hands lay, in a relaxed manner, on your thigh just above your knee. Allow your body to relax and gaze at your hand. Give yourself the following thoughts: "My hand is getting very, very light. In a moment it will become lighter than air. It will become buoyant and begin to float in the air. My hand is getting lighter and lighter. It feels as light as a feather. My hand feels like a leaf being blown by a brisk autumn breeze." When your hand begins to rise, tell yourself: "My hand continues to get lighter and lighter, and it will continue to rise until I say the word, 'NOW.'"

This test will involve more time than the others, but if you succeed with this one, you are indeed doing well.

The next few tests rely almost entirely on the imagination. The first five tests used the imagination, but there were also strong physical factors involved. Now we are placing the emphasis on the imagination and your ability to create mental images.

Test Six. If possible, lie on your back for this mental exercise. Close your eyes and begin to remember a meal you have eaten recently, preferably a special meal where there were lots of people. Take your time; let your mind slowly drift back to the occasion. See yourself seated at the table. See the table, the tablecloth, the dinnerware, the silverware, the glassware; see the other people and the room itself. Now begin to *feel* yourself seated at the table. Begin to *relive* this meal. See the food, etc. Feel the silverware. Hear the clinking of the dishes. Hear the conversation. Taste the food. Smell the food. Take your time and relive the entire meal. If reliving a meal doesn't appeal to your imagination, relive any incident you wish.

Those who respond well to this test will be able to attain self-hypnosis in a very short time.

Test Seven. Make yourself comfortable in either a sitting or prone position. Close your eyes and begin to visualize a house, any house that appeals to you. Imagine you are seeing this house in the distance. See it in three dimensions. Take your time and allow the house and surrounding scenery to come into focus. In a few minutes the house and scenery will begin to take shape and form. At this point begin to visualize the coloring of the landscape, of the sky, and of the house itself. Give yourself time and it will come to you. If there is anything peculiar or different about the house, notice it, see it. Now see yourself walking toward the house. Open the door and enter. Go into some of the various rooms of this house and see the furniture, drapes, etc.

If seeing a house doesn't appeal to you, see anything you wish —a school, store, church, etc.

Not everyone will respond completely to this test, so do not worry if you can't see the house in three dimensions or if you can't visualize the colors. Any positive response to the test is in your favor as far as self-hypnosis is concerned.

Test Eight. Close your eyes and visualize a black dot in the middle of your forehead. Take your time and allow it to materialize. When the black dot appears, see a red circle form around it, then a blue circle, etc. until all the colors you can think of have encircled it.

This next test entails the use of a physiological response, which will amaze some of you.

Test Nine. While seated allow your hand to lay in your lap. You may keep your eyes open and look at your hand or you may close them. Give yourself the following thoughts: "My hand is beginning to tingle. It is beginning to get numb and frozen. My hand feels as though little needles are pricking it all over. My hand is getting colder and colder, and in just a moment it will be so numb and frozen it will be insensitive to pain. All sense of feeling is leaving my hand and in just a moment my hand will be completely numb and frozen. In fact, when I count to three, my hand will be completely numb and frozen and insensitive until I say the word, 'NOW.' When I count to three, I will pinch myself. I will feel some pressure, but that is all. My hand will feel comfortable when I pinch it."

If you will take your time when trying these tests, you will succeed with many of them. Being relaxed and using the imagination is of the utmost importance.

Those of you who respond to six or more of these tests will make wonderful, quick, and easy progress in self-hypnosis, provided you apply yourself diligently to the task.

Those who responded well to two to five of the tests will also find it relatively simple to achieve self-hypnosis.

If you only responded to one or two tests, do not be discouraged, because any response is a good response. If you didn't respond to any of the tests, this doesn't mean you can't achieve self-hypnosis. I have given you only nine tests. There are, of course, many others which space doesn't permit, and I am sure you would respond to one of them. In fact, I believe that everyone will respond in some measure to one or all of these tests. For instance, maybe your hands didn't get so heavy in Test Four that you couldn't lift them, but they did feel heavier than they were. This would not be a total response, but it is a positive response. Perhaps in Test Seven, you couldn't see a house in three dimensions or in color, but you could think of a particular house. This is also a positive response.

Practice these suggestion tests at least once before proceeding further in the book. For the next month or two practice a different test every day until you become proficient at them. By doing this you will be developing the basic tools which will enable you to be effective in the use of self-hypnosis. This is the foundation; build it well.

HIGHLIGHTS TO REMEMBER FROM THIS CHAPTER:

1. If you are to learn self-hypnosis you must apply yourself to the task.
2. At first, you will need to practice at least fifteen minutes a day.
3. The best and quickest way to learn self-hypnosis is with the aid of a professional hypnotist.
4. Recordings can be an invaluable aid to you in learning self-hypnosis.
5. Although a hypnotist and recordings facilitate matters, it is still possible to learn self-hypnosis on your own.
6. The hindrances you need to avoid in learning self-hypnosis are:
   (1) Not recognizing the state of hypnosis. Most people who get hypnotized don't think they are in hypnosis. Review Chapter 2.
   (2) An "overly analytical" attitude.
   (3) The "prove it to me" attitude.
   (4) Avoid "trying too hard."
7. Give yourself time to learn self-hypnosis. Don't expect miracles overnight. Begin as a beginner.
8. If possible, practice at the same time and place every day. Have someone answer the door and phone for you.
9. Try the nine suggestion tests before proceeding further in the book.
10. Don't be discouraged.

5

HOW TO HYPNOTIZE
YOURSELF SUCCESSFULLY

LET'S GET DOWN TO BUSINESS! By now, you should have a pretty good basic idea as to how hypnosis works. Whatever fears you had should be gone. You should also know, from the suggestion tests given in the last chapter, in what way you are the most suggestible.

TWO BASICS TO REMEMBER

There are two things which you should keep in mind at this point: All hypnosis is self-hypnosis, and your basic tools are suggestion and imagination. In order to hypnotize yourself, you must become your own hypnotist. This means you will give yourself suggestions and appeal to your own imagination.

At first, this can be done in two ways. You can give yourself the suggestions by memorizing or familiarizing yourself with the hypnotic formulas you will find in the latter part of this chapter and thinking them to yourself! Or you can put them on tape and listen to your own voice on the tape recorder. The tape recorder makes it literally possible for you to become your own hypnotist. Use the tape recorder as a temporary measure to teach yourself self-hypnosis. This doesn't mean you shouldn't use the recorder in the future, but don't make it a substitute for self-hypnosis. You can't always carry a tape recorder with you, and situations will arise where you will want to give yourself instant self-hypnotic suggestions.

If you decide to make use of a tape recorder, read the hypnotic formulas into the tape recorder with a clear resonant voice. Read slowly, with feeling.

If you are going to proceed by thinking the suggestions, you should decide which formula you are going to use and then read it repeatedly until you are thoroughly acquainted with the thoughts contained in the formula. When you are ready to hypnotize yourself, merely think these thoughts. At the same time you are thinking you should feel what you are thinking. Take your time. Don't rush. Allow enough time for your nervous system to react to your suggestions.

SELECTING YOUR BEST BASIS OF HYPNOTIC RESPONSE

Before giving you the hypnotic formulas, I would like to mention this. You may take any of the tests to which you responded well in the last chapter and use it to induce self-hypnosis. When you hypnotize yourself, you narrow your attention span to primarily one thing. This is usually done by the proper use of your imagination. For example, in the first test of the last chapter you were to make your thumb and middle finger stick together by imagining they were glued and taped together. Once you have accomplished this, tell yourself your eyes are going to become heavy and close, and that you are going into the state of hypnosis. From this point begin to use one of the hypnotic formulas given in this chapter.

If you responded well to the fifth test, tell yourself that your hand will float to your cheek, and when it touches your cheek, your eyes will close, and you will go into hypnosis. At that time use one of the hypnotic formulas of this chapter.

I think you can see by these two illustrations that, when you can control one part of your body or mind, you can use that as a bridge to control another part and eventually enter into hypnosis. Once you fully comprehend this fact you have won half the battle.

If you use a tape recorder, follow the same procedure, except that once you respond to the test you will have someone turn on the tape recorder at a given signal.

I have used only two tests as examples, but you utilize the same technique with any of the tests. Remember that, as soon as you respond to the test, you then tell yourself you are going into hypnosis. At this point begin to use one of the hypnotic formulas to further and complete the hypnosis. If you prefer, you may use the hypnotic formulas by themselves. They will prove to be more than sufficient to put you into hypnosis.

This particular technique has been my favorite for hypnotizing others. Once I learn how they respond to suggestion, I proceed from there to place them into deep hypnosis.

All of the hypnotic formulas given in this chapter can be divided into four sections. The first part contains the induction, and the second part, the deepening process. The third section is the actual suggestion given for the post-hypnotic response. The fourth part is the so-called awakening procedure. The formula which follows is called the progressive relaxation technique:

HYPNOTIC FORMULA 1

"As I close my eyes, I enter into a complete state of relaxation. I pay attention only to the thoughts I am giving myself. Any noises or sounds I might hear will not distract or disturb me. In fact, they will actually deepen my hypnosis. Each time I go into hypnosis, I will go into it more deeply and quickly than the previous time. I now feel perfectly comfortable and at ease. My breathing is easy, normal, and gentle. Every breath I take puts me more deeply into hypnosis. I feel the stream of air in my nostrils, and every breath I take puts me more and more deeply into relaxation. I feel my pulse beat, and every beat of my pulse puts me more and more deeply into relaxation.

"I now center my attention on my right foot. I center my attention on my right foot. My right foot begins to relax. The muscles in my toes begin to relax. The muscles in my toes relax more and more. This relaxing feeling moves into the arch of my foot and into my heel. My entire right foot feels enveloped in relaxation. My right foot is loose and limp and totally and completely relaxed. It has the sensation that it is being gently massaged.

"Now I center my attention on my left foot. My left foot begins to relax. My left foot is relaxing more and more. The muscles in my left foot become loose and limp. The toes of my left foot relax. This sensation moves up into the ball of my foot, the arch, and the heel of my foot. This relaxation encompasses my foot completely. My left foot is totally and completely relaxed.

"This relaxing sensation moves into my ankles, and they become relaxed and limp. The joints of my ankles become loose and relaxed.

"This sensation of relaxation moves into my calves, and my calves become limp and relaxed. They too feel as though they are being gently massaged. They become completely and fully relaxed. They are relaxed.

"This relaxation moves into my knees, and my knees become fully relaxed. All strain is gone. This dynamic relaxation moves into my thighs, and they become loose and limp. The muscles, tendons, and joints become limp and fully relaxed.

"I am going deeper and deeper with every breath I take.

"This relaxing sensation reaches up into my hips and the pelvic region of my body. These muscles become totally relaxed. They become limp and relaxed. This relaxation moves up into my abdomen. It proceeds into my back. The muscles and nerves in my back and abdomen become completely and fully relaxed. Every breath I take puts me more deeply into relaxation. It feels as though someone is giving me a gentle massage. This relaxation spreads to both my chest and upper back. It goes around and relaxes the chest and back muscles totally. I am becoming more and more relaxed.

"This dynamic relaxation now moves to the tips of my fingers, on into my hands and into my wrists; it now slowly and gently proceeds into my forearms. They are loose and limp and completely relaxed. This sensation of relaxation moves up into my elbows; they become relaxed; the joints and muscles relax. This relaxation now proceeds into my upper arms. All of the biceps and triceps become relaxed. This glowing, wonderful relaxation moves into the deltoid muscles of my shoulders and on into my neck muscles and relaxes my spinal column. It feels as though someone is gently, yet vigorously, massaging my spinal column, and this gentle massaging further relaxes all the muscles in my body.

"It now feels as though someone is gently kneading the muscles of my neck and along the tip of my shoulders; my neck and shoulders are relaxing more and more. My whole body continues to go deeper and deeper into relaxation. This relaxation goes around and gently caresses my throat. My throat feels comfortable and relaxed. This wonderful soothing relaxation now creeps up the back of my head and goes over the top of my head. The top of my head is so relaxed that the scalp feels loose. I am relaxing more and more and going deeper and deeper into hypnosis. Now this wonderful relaxation moves gently down over my face. My forehead becomes relaxed and a pleasant cool feeling bathes my forehead. My jaws are relaxing. They are relaxing so much my teeth come slightly apart. My eyelids relax. All the muscles and nerves which control the movements of my eyelids relax. They are so relaxed that they feel like soft rubber bands thrown upon a table.

"My whole body is now relaxed and will continue to relax more and more throughout this time of self-hypnosis. My body is so relaxed that it feels boneless. It feels as though there isn't a bone in my body.

"My mind has been relaxing with my body. My mind is experiencing a wonderful sense of peace and tranquility. All tension, worry, doubt and fear leave me. My subconscious is now becoming receptive to good thoughts and ideas which I will soon give myself.

"I am now going deeper and deeper into relaxation. As I count from ten backwards to zero I will go deeper with every number that I count. Ten—I am relaxing more and more, and I am going deeper and deeper. Nine—I just let go and go deeper and deeper into this wonderful relaxation. Eight—all tension and strain leave my body, and I go deeper and deeper. Seven—down and down, deeper and deeper. Six—I relax more and more and go deeper and deeper. Five—down and down and deeper and deeper. Four —deeper and deeper. Three—down and down. Two—down and down—deeper and deeper. One—deep, deep, deep, deep relaxation. Zero—now I am totally and completely relaxed, and my subconscious is now ready to receive suggestions."

SUPPLEMENTARY SUGGESTIONS
AND AWAKENING PROCEDURES

"In the future I will never accidentally fall into hypnosis. I will never be hypnotized when driving a motor vehicle or when operating any dangerous equipment. When I do wish to hypnotize myself in the future, all I will have to do is make myself comfortable and say, "Relax now, relax now, relax now" to myself. When I say these words to myself I will immediately go into hypnosis. Each time I hypnotize myself I get better at it. Each time I will go into hypnosis more deeply and quickly than the previous time. Each time I hypnotize myself I will automatically achieve the proper balance between the conscious mind and the subconscious, so that I can effectively give myself suggestions. These suggestions are now sinking deep, deep into my subconscious. My subconscious will automatically feed these thoughts back into my conscious life."

Once you have become effective with your self-hypnosis, you may add any suggestion you wish.

"Now I am going to return to a normal state of consciousness. When I awaken, I will feel wonderful. My mind will be alert, and my body will be fully coordinated. I will feel full of vim, vigor, and vitality. I will feel refreshed and revived. I will be completely normal in every way. I now count to five, and when I get to five I will be fully awake. One—I am awakening. Two—all heavy feeling leaves my body. Three—I am getting more and more awake, and I feel wonderful. Four—my eyes open. Five—I take a deep breath, and I am completely awake."

The following induction will work especially well with those who find it easy to create mental images:

HYPNOTIC FORMULA 2

"As I close my eyes I go into a wonderful, deep state of relaxation, and I become more and more relaxed with every breath I take. I feel the stream of air going into my nostrils, and I go deeper with every breath I take. I feel my heart beat, and I go deeper with every beat of my heart. I feel my pulse beat, and I go deeper with every beat of my pulse. Every breath I take puts me deeper into relaxation.

"I see myself walking along a beautiful, sandy beach. I see myself walking along a beautiful, sandy beach. I am barefooted. I am barefooted, and I feel the warm sand between my toes. (Pause and allow yourself time to feel the sand between your toes.) As I walk along the beach, I am becoming more and more tired. I am becoming comfortably tired. Off to one side I see a huge sand dune. Off to one side, I see a huge sand dune. On top of this sand dune, I see two large, beautiful pine trees. Between the two pine trees is a hammock swinging gently in the breeze. Next to the trunk of one of the trees is a bottle of cool, refreshing water.

"Because I am so tired, and since I am so thirsty, I will climb to the top of this huge sand dune. When I get to the top, I will take a drink of water. Then I will get into the hammock and go into the deepest state of relaxation possible for me at this time. When I get into the hammock, I will go into the deepest state of relaxation possible for me at this time.

"I now start to run, and I run. My legs become so tired that they momentarily give out on me. I fall on my hands and knees. I see myself with my hands and knees in the sand. I feel the sand oozing between my fingers. I feel the sand under my knees. My knees are buried in the sand. I feel the sand oozing between my toes. I am becoming more and more comfortably tired, and I can hardly wait until I get to the top of the sand dune, so I can get into the hammock and go into the deepest relaxation possible for me at this time. I now get up and proceed up the sand dune. As I go up the side of the sand hill, I am becoming more and more comfortably tired. My legs become tired and feel like lumps of lead. My arms become tired and feel like lumps of lead. The trunk of my body becomes tired and feels like a lump of lead. My head becomes tired and feels like a lump of lead. My whole body feels comfortably heavy and tired.

"I slowly walk up and up until I reach the top of the sand hill. I slowly walk up and up until I reach the top of the sand dune. I am almost at the top. I am almost at the top. I am getting closer and closer. I am getting closer and closer. I am on top of the sand dune. I am on top of the sand dune. Now I take a cool re-freshing drink of water. I take a cool refreshing drink of water.

"I am now climbing into the hammock. I am climbing into the hammock. I get into the hammock. I stretch out and go into a deep state of relaxation. I am now in the deepest state of relaxation possible for me at this time. As I lie in this comfortable hammock, I feel waves of relaxation surging through my body.

"I feel a gentle, pleasant, cool breeze caressing my body. I feel this cool breeze going over my face and shoulders. It blows across my chest and abdomen. I feel its relaxing effect on my legs and feet. I am relaxing more and more and going deeper and deeper than ever before into deep, deep, deep relaxation.

"I feel the hammock being gently blown in the breeze. It sways back and forth and back and forth. As it sways back and forth, I feel myself relaxing more and more and more and more. As it sways back and forth I count backwards from ten to zero, and I go even deeper into hypnosis. Ten—as I continue to relax more and more all the tensions and cares of the day leave me. Nine—as I go deeper and deeper I feel myself in deep communion with God. I am very aware of His presence. Eight—deeper and deeper on down. Seven—I just let go and go deeper and deeper than ever before. Six—my mind and body are becoming totally and completely relaxed. Five—deeper and deeper on down. Four—down and down—down and down. Three—I let go more and more and go deeper and deeper. Two—oo-oo-oo . . . One—un-un-un . . . Zero—deep, deep, deep hypnosis, deeper than ever before."

At this point use the suggestions and awakening procedure found at the end of the first induction.

HYPNOTIC FORMULA 3

The following induction is a wonderful induction for religious people. It is very effective in strengthening their faith and devotion to God:

"I close my eyes, and as I close them, I feel myself beginning to relax. I am relaxing more and more, and soon I will be in the deepest state of relaxation possible for me at this time. As I relax, I am becoming more and more aware of my mind and less and less aware of my body. I am also very cognizant of the fact that God wants me to control my body and emotions instead of my body and emotions controlling me. I now rest deeply,—body, soul, and spirit in the peace of God. As I rest in His love I feel myself relaxing totally and completely. In my mind I see a cross. (People who are of non-Christian faiths should substitute a religious symbol which is in accordance with their belief.) From this cross emanate waves of God's love and grace which brings me peace and relaxation. I feel perfectly comfortable and secure in the love of God. These waves from the cross bring faith, peace, and healing to my body, soul, and spirit. I am becoming more and more relaxed. As I become more and more relaxed, I become more and more aware of God's presence within me.

"All fear is leaving me and is being replaced with dynamic faith. All pessimism is leaving me and is being replaced with optimism. All depression and despair are leaving me and are being replaced with glorious hope and boundless joy. All hatred and bitterness are leaving me and are being replaced with unselfish love.

"As I relax more and more, God becomes real in my life. I realize that His power, love, grace, peace, mercy, and forgiveness are always at my disposal.

"With this wonderful knowledge and peace in my mind, I now count from ten to zero to deepen my relaxation. Ten—deeper and deeper. Nine—I continue to feel the waves of God's love and grace from the cross and go deeper and deeper. Eight—every particle of my body is relaxing totally and completely. Seven—deeper and deeper and deeper down. Six—down and down—deeper and down. Five—I just let go and go deeper. Four— . . . Three—e-e-e- . . . Two—oo-oo-oo- . . . One—un-un-un . . . Zero—o-o-o."

At this point use the suggestions and awakening procedures found at the end of the first hypnotic induction formula.

There are hundreds of hypnotic inductions, but I have selected these three because I find they work with most people. Now that you have the idea, formulate your own induction if you wish. These inductions and formulas will work if you will allow them to work.

HIGHLIGHTS TO REMEMBER FROM THIS CHAPTER:

1. The basic tools of hypnosis are suggestion and imagination.
2. You may use the induction formulas of this chapter in two ways: You may memorize and think them or you may read them into a tape recorder and listen to them.

3. Take any of the tests to which you respond in Chapter 4 and use them as induction techniques.
4. Formula 1—Relaxation Technique.
5. Formula 2—Visual Imagery Technique.
6. Formula 3—Religious Technique.

the imagination can hinder a student. Now, I am going to give you a very personal story of how the proper use of the imagination helped one of my sons in a very remarkable way. My second son, Blair, had experienced a difficult time in school right from the beginning. When he was in the first term of the first grade, his marks were just barely above the failure level. This was a terrific burden to me, because I was helping other children, but I couldn't seem to get through to my own son. We sent him to the school psychologist for an interview and testings, and he informed us that his intelligence was above average.

One morning, after completing breakfast, Blair said to me, "Daddy, I have a test today, could you help me to be smart for the test?" As a spontaneous reaction, I placed my hands on his head, and told him his thinking cap was coming on, and he would be completely relaxed while taking his test. I also told him he would be able to remember everything he had ever learned. Really, my wife and I didn't think too much about it. In fact, we kind of laughed at the way Blair seemed to be in a trance when I did this. But when I came home that evening my wife and Blair were overwhelmed with joy: Blair had received an "A" on his exam. Needless to say, I placed Blair's "thinking cap" on his head every day for about two months. Then I started putting it on every other day, then twice a week, once a week, and finally I told him it was on forever. Blair, since that time, has had no major problem with his studies. He is a typical boy, who gets a little lazy and doesn't want to do his studies, but there has been a definite change in his mind power.

In conjunction with this I would like to mention the wonderful manner in which the school psychologist handled Blair. About two months after I started putting the "thinking cap" on him, the psychologist called Blair in for an interview. And during the interview he told Blair that he had a "smart brain." This thrilled Blair no end and greatly increased his confidence. I think that this, along with the "thinking cap," were the two things which changed his mental life.

IMAGINATION TO INDUCE SELF-HYPNOSIS

In an earlier chapter, I mentioned that suggestion is the avenue which leads to hypnosis, but imagination is the vehicle in which you ride. You can use imagination to induce self-hypnosis. It is very effective if you desire to do nothing more than relax the mind and body. Imagination is also the best tool to use in deepening your hypnosis. The applications of these facts are too numerous to mention them all.

HOW ONE PERSON QUIT SMOKING

Your imagination can also help you realize your goals. I had been working, without success, with a young man who was trying to quit cigarettes. He was a good subject, he had strong motivation, and it seemed as though he should be able to stop, but he couldn't! I racked my brain trying to figure out why I had failed, but I couldn't find the answer. Finally, after eight sessions, I told him that, if he didn't make any improvement by the next week, I wouldn't feel right in taking his money. He returned the next week with a big smile on his face and informed me that he had "quit." Then he proceeded to unfold how he had quit.

I had taught him a technique of self-hypnosis in which he wrote his suggestion on a piece of paper, then summarized the entire suggestion in one word. He then induced self-hypnosis and let this word float in his mind for three or four minutes. Finally, he would count to five and awaken. He did this for seven weeks without any consequential results. But throughout this last week, he used his imagination while under hypnosis. His key summary word for his suggestion to cease smoking was "stop." Instead of merely letting the word "stop" float in his mind, he visualized a stop sign with a cigarette painted across it! This did the trick! He stopped smoking because he combined his imagination with hypnosis.

HOW TO INCREASE THE POWER
OF YOUR IMAGINATION

Let me now give a few pointers on how to increase the power of your imagination. *First*, you must recognize the power of your imagination. This is essential! If you don't fully grasp this fact, you will never realize your full potential in life. *Second*, learn to control your imagination. Set aside a few minutes each day and practice seeing visual images in your mind. Imagine light or heavy hands, feet, etc . . . *Third*, learn to always use your imagination as a preparation for constructive activity. Never use it for idle daydreaming. Learn to control it and direct it for beneficial purposes. *Fourth,* begin to develop the creative aspect of your imagination. Visualize new products and new services which would be of great value to mankind. Think of new approach procedures and techniques for the advancement of your business or your way of life. *Fifth,* when you seem to be up against a wall, let your imagination run wild. Some call this "brain-storming." From these "wild thoughts" will come some "solution thoughts." Sixth, keep on practicing until you can effectively use your imagination for your benefit.

HIGHLIGHTS TO REMEMBER FROM THIS CHAPTER:

1. Your imagination can make you or break you.
2. The real secret of success is a creative imagination.
3. We are all born with good imaginations. You still have an imagination, even though it might be dormant and inactive.
4. Your imagination is more powerful than your "will power."
5. All great accomplishments begin as an idea.
6. Your imagination, if misused, can hinder you.
7. Your imagination, if misused, can undermine you. It is important that you distinguish between idle daydreaming and constructive imagination. Creative imagination is always productive.
8. Your imagination, if misused, can destroy you.
9. Your imagination can help you increase your income and improve your human relationships and your school grades.
10. Your imagination can help you to be more effective in inducing and deepening your self-hypnosis.
11. Your imagination can help you realize your goals when combined with self-hypnosis.
12. A step-by-step program to help you better utilize your imagination:
    (1) Recognize its value and power.
    (2) Learn to control it.
    (3) Use it as a preparation for constructive activity.
    (4) Develop the creative aspect of your imagination.
    (5) At times, let it run wild.
    (6) Practice makes perfect.

9

BASIC DYNAMICS
OF EFFECTIVE SUGGESTION
(YOUR P.D.E.M.)

KNOWING HOW TO WORD A suggestion properly is just as important, or perhaps more important, than a deep hypnotic trance as far as achieving results is concerned. Of what value is it to learn how to relax if you don't know how to give yourself the proper suggestion while in hypnosis? You will, of course, receive great benefits from the state of physical and mental relaxation. A great number of people seek my services for this one thing; to learn how to relax. But if you desire to receive improvement in some particular area of your life, it is imperative that you have a thorough knowledge of the basic rules of suggestion.

I have found that when I finally write a suggestion which appeals to me and fits my need, often this is all that is necessary to achieve the improvement I desire. It takes much thought and self-examination in order to frame a suggestion which will help you realize your goal. During the time you are writing and rewriting your suggestion, you are convincing your subconscious of your desire, and once in awhile this is sufficient to bring about the desired improvement.

THE SIX GREAT PRINCIPLES OF EFFECTIVE SUGGESTION

Now let us consider the six great principles of suggestion. If we add to them the fact that the subconscious is a "goal-striving mechanism," we will have seven great rules of suggestion to help you in your progress.

Basically, three of the principles in this chapter are those set forth by the famous Emile Coue. I have added a few of my ideas to them, but all humanity should be grateful to Emile Coue for his wonderful genius. The other principles we will discuss are based on findings revealed by Jerome D. Frank, M.D., in his book *Persuasion and Healing*.

PRINCIPLE 1
THE LAW OF THE POSITIVE DOMINANT
EMOTIONAL MOTIVATOR

Man, among other things, is an emotional being. The average person's behavior is governed more by his emotions than by his intellect. "Feelings," the result of emotions, are the prime movers among human beings. Advertisers are well aware of this fact. Very seldom do they make an appeal to the intellect—their appeal is always to the emotions. The amazing thing about this is that very few intelligent people take the time to really evaluate a product. They accept the emotional appeal and believe it.

Every good salesman knows how to appeal to the emotions. How successful would a vacuum sweeper salesman be if he directed his sales appeal to the housewive's intellect? "Mrs. Brown, this sweeper has a three-quarter horsepower motor which generates x number of r.p.m.'s per minute. The waste container has a capacity of three gallons and is made out of the best nylon. The main hose attachment is ten feet long . . ." A vacuum sweeper salesman with this approach would starve to death. But if he makes an emotional approach he will sell. "Mrs. Brown, I know you already have a vacuum, and you have just used it on your carpet. This will help me demonstrate this fine machine which I am selling." He then proceeds to vacuum the floor, and takes up a sizeable amount of dirt, which any other vacuum would also do. But the young mother and housewife doesn't realize this, and immediately *feels* badly because there is dirt in her rug. She wants to keep a clean house. Then the salesman says, "Mrs. Brown, I know you want to have the cleanest house possible, but you can't do it with your present sweeper. Also, think of your little baby crawling and playing on this carpet with all the germs it contains . . ." With this emotional approach the salesman will sell.

You might say, "This wouldn't work with me. I am a hardheaded business man, and no one can sell me with an emotional pitch." Please, don't deceive yourself with this type of thinking. Everyone has emotions, and everyone is motivated by his or her emotions. One of the best stories I ever heard vividly illustrates this fact. It was told to me by an insurance salesman. A friend of his, who was representing an insurance firm in a small Mid-Western town, was trying desperately to sell a client some life insurance. This client was one of the few wealthy men in the town, and he already possessed $75,000 worth of life insurance. The salesman was endeavoring to have him purchase another $25,000 policy to bring his total protection to $100,000. His approach had been intellectual and realistic but to no avail. The gentleman just wasn't interested in any more life insurance. As the salesman started to leave, his client asked him where he had gotten the beautiful gold button with the number 100 engraved on it. The salesman had received this button for selling $100,000 worth of insurance in three months. But this isn't what he told the client! He told the client his company was going to give one of these buttons to every man in town who owned $100,000 worth of insurance. And only four other people in town could afford to wear one. He had worn the button on his coat because he thought he would sell him the $25,000 policy and give him the button. When the client heard that this gold pin was a mark of distinction, and only four other men in town could afford one, he bought the extra insurance. A one dollar gold-plated button, plus a strong prestige appeal, sold the insurance.

Emotions are man's strongest motivators. Every habit, every behavior pattern receives its impetus from emotion. The secret of success and happiness in life is to be able to direct and to some degree control one's emotions.

Whenever a conflict exists in your life, the dominant emotion will win. You want to launch out in your work, but you are afraid. Which emotion will win: your desire for advancement (pride, self-preservation, prestige, etc.) or fear? The answer to this would of course depend on your psychological make-up. One thing for certain, however, is that one of these feelings will be dominant and this will be the determining factor. You have a terrific headache until your husband comes home and tells you he just received a $500 bonus. When you hear this news you forget all about the headache. The dominant emotion of joy overcomes whatever emotion it was that induced your headache.

I have known a number of people who have tried to stop smoking, but who failed. Then they went to their physician for a checkup and he told them, "You'd better give up smoking or you are going to die." After this, they didn't have too much trouble in their effort to stop smoking. To me this is a poor motivator, but it is quite effective with most people. In this example fear dominates pleasure.

Why you must find your dominant emotional factor: If you wish to improve a particular aspect of your life, or change a habit, or overcome a hindrance you must find a dominant emotional motivator which will be stronger than the emotion which now dominates you. The very fact that you desire to effect a change in this area of your life implies that the present dominant emotional motivator is a negative force in your life. This is true, although the motivator under other circumstances would be considered positive. An individual who overeats might be doing this because of the pleasure he derives from food. There is nothing negative about pleasure in itself, but when it brings harm to the body, as in the case of an excessive eater, then I consider it a negative, dominant, emotional motivator.

The problem then is to search your heart, mind, and soul for a positive dominant emotional motivator which will dethrone the negative motivator. For the sake of brevity, I will refer to the positive dominant emotional motivator as the P.D.E.M. My students are always discussing their P.D.E.M.'s.

How to find your P.D.E.M.: The only way you can determine an effective P.D.E.M. for your desired goal is to be completely honest with yourself. This is more difficult than it seems, because I have discovered that few people are honest with themselves.

We all have a tendency to rationalize, project, or repress our feelings, but if we want to succeed with our self-hypnosis we must be perfectly candid with ourselves when probing for our P.D.E.M.

In one of my classes, we were discussing various P.D.E.M.'s which would direct the individual toward success. Many of the common motivations were given—money, helping others, more leisure time to devote to creative efforts, money for the children's education . . . Then one man, who already was quite successful, shocked the class by saying his strongest motivation in this area would be a desire to dominate others. He liked to be boss; he wanted to be "top dog." As I said, this shocked the class, but I believe he was one of the few who were really being honest. His P.D.E.M. certainly wasn't what you would call altruistic, nor would you deem it exactly moral, but it would fulfill his ambitions.

When deciding on a P.D.E.M., scan your mind and try to determine what makes you tick. Do you want that advancement at work, because of financial gain, prestige, the strengthening of your wife's esteem for you, etc.? Just what is the reason? It might be one of these or all of them, plus others. It is best to choose the strongest one, but sometimes two or three will be needed.

If you want to get better marks in school, ask yourself what is your strongest P.D.E.M. for doing so. Is it because you want the feeling of personal satisfaction or a good position after graduation or the approval of your parents? Determine as much as possible exactly what it is.

Sometimes your P.D.E.M. will be so definite and so powerful you won't have to write it as part of your suggestion. At other times it will be the determining factor as to your success. When this is the case, be sure to write it into your suggestion. Regardless of the situation, always emotionalize your self-hypnosis with your P.D.E.M.

PRINCIPLE 2
THE LAW OF SELF-APPROVAL

For a number of years psychologists have conducted experiments with animals utilizing a technique known as "operant conditioning." The procedure involves the immediate rewarding of the animal or bird when his behavior complies with the wishes of the psychologists. It has been found that this greatly increases the learning process with animals. A mouse confined to a cage with ten openings will try all of them, but every time he goes to the right one he receives a piece of cheese. When this process is repeated often enough, it can become a fixed pattern. The animal responds because of the reward he receives. This reward is also a symbol of the psychologist's approval. Based upon these findings similar experiments were conducted with humans. The rewards received by humans were in the form of words and gestures. An individual might be told to say numbers, any numbers he wanted, and there didn't have to be a particular order. Every time he would say a number with "5" in it, the operator would make a slight sound of approval. As a result of this approval the person in the experiment would repeat numbers with "5" in them more than any other number. He does this even though he doesn't know the real purpose of the experiment. He is completely unaware of what is taking place.

I have gone into a little detail here to show you the scientific basis of this law: the law of self-approval. We are all concerned, to various degrees, about what others think about us. We want their approval. This begins with childhood, when we want the approval of our parents. And it continues throughout our life.

How self-approval is related to effective self-hypnosis: There is one thing, however, which is more important to you than the approval of others and that is the approval of yourself. In order to have peace of mind and emotional equilibrium you must approve of yourself.

This fact is related to self-hypnosis in the sense that a suggestion will not be effective with you if it is contrary to a deep moral conviction. For instance, you might outwardly desire a greater degree of financial success, but inwardly you harbor the belief that money is basically evil. Before a suggestion concerning financial success would ever bring results in your life, you would have to re-educate your inner belief in regard to money.

I was raised during the hard, lean years of the depression. My parents were poor people. We never went hungry, and we weren't deprived of the necessities of life, but we had very few of the luxuries. It was the consensus of all of the people with whom I was raised that any man with wealth was crooked. You just couldn't be honest and have money. As I look back on those years, it is easy for me to understand why those people felt as they did, for they had very little of anything, including hope.

This belief which I acquired in the early years of my life stayed with me for a long period of time. Actually, I wasn't able to change it until I recognized that I possessed it. When I was working in an automobile factory one summer, I noticed that every time I received a check above a certain amount I felt guilty and afraid. As I analyzed my feelings I knew it was a result of the influence of my early years.

Asserting self-confidence: Another area where this condition often exists is in the area of self-confidence and self-expression. Outwardly you want confidence, yet inwardly you feel it would not really be right for you to express your opinion to someone you consider your superior. To a degree this is true of all of us because we have been taught that "children are to be seen but not heard." Don't talk back to the teacher, the policeman, etc. This is good advice when you are a child, but it can be a hindrance when you enter the adult world. Some individuals find it very difficult to overcome this inner attitude because of the rigid training of their youth. You will never be competent in expressing yourself until you resolve this conflict of thought.

Work, especially hard work, is right and good, but ease and pleasure are evil and sinful—or so we have been taught. This inner belief creates some real problems for people about to retire. They want to retire, but they feel guilty about not working. If you were to give yourself the self-hypnosis suggestion "I want to retire at the age of 45 or 50" while entertaining this inner belief, you would not be very successful.

Outwardly you might want to be popular with the opposite sex, yet inwardly you might feel all relationships with them are sinful. You could give yourself suggestion after suggestion in regard to this matter, but you would never be completely effective until you had resolved this inner belief.

When writing your self-hypnosis suggestion be sure they meet the demands of your self-approval. If you are aware of an inner belief which will be detrimental to the fulfillment of your goal, resolve it by re-education. This can be done on both a conscious and subconscious level.

PRINCIPLE 3
THE LAW OF REVERSED EFFECT

The law of reversed effect is this: Whenever you endeavor to make a change in your life by the means of a conscious effort you will not succeed. In fact, you will actually strengthen the habit or idea you wish to change. For instance, the more you try to go to sleep at night, the more you stay awake. The more you try to remember something, the less apt you are to remember it. The more you try to remove an idea or thought from your mind, the more entrenched it becomes.

Weaknesses of negative statements: Whenever a negative thought is added to your effort, you completely ruin your chances of success: "I will not be afraid." "I will not eat too much." "I will not want to smoke." "I will not forget." "I will not lose my temper." Statements such as these are self-defeating. They plant a negative vacuum in the mind. You will not be afraid, but what will you be? You will not eat too much, but how much will you eat? You will not smoke, but what will take the place of smoking in your life? It is most important that you frame your suggestion in a positive manner. If possible, never use a negation in forming your suggestion.

Another weakness of a negative statement is that it mentions the things you wish to change and makes a direct appeal to the imagination. When you declare, "I will not be afraid," you immediately form the image of fear in your mind. As a result of this, fear becomes the predominant factor in your thoughts. How much better it would be for you to say, "I will be calm and confident at all times and in all situations." When you make this affirmation, your mind perceives the image you desire it to see. You see yourself being confident and calm no matter what happens.

Whenever you make a negative statement to yourself or anyone else, it is like waving a red cape in front of a bull. The word "don't" is a challenge to most people. Many times it is an idea!

Mother says, "Johnny don't walk through the mud." Well, maybe Johnny hadn't even thought of walking through the mud (although, I grant you this is very unlikely). Nonetheless, as the result of his mother's statement, a wonderful idea appears in little Johnny's mind—MUD. He quickly forgets the "don't," but he remembers the words, "walk through the mud." I am confident every mother reading this has had a similar experience with her child.

All of us have somewhat of a spirit of rebellion within us, and when someone tells us not to do something we invariably want to show him that we do as we please. We don't have to take orders from anyone. We will show him! If the individual's authority over us is not great, we probably will defy him and do just the opposite of what he wants us to do. If his authority is absolute, we will conform outwardly, but inwardly our soul and emotions will be in a state of smoldering rebellion. This should be a word to the wise for every parent, teacher, or anyone else who has the responsibility of handling and directing people. The individual who commands others "not to do this or not to do that" might achieve some good short term results, but in the long run he will not succeed.

Before proceeding further let me summarize the three weaknesses of a negative suggestion.

1. It creates a vacuum. It doesn't tell you what to do.
2. It produces the wrong mental imagery. You think of the thing you want to change.
3. It poses a challenge. This is true even when you are giving yourself a suggestion. "I enjoy this habit, why does it have to be harmful?"

I believe the religious philosophy of "touch not, taste not, and see not," causes more emotional and spiritual problems than any other one thing. It presumes that living a life of negation has some meritorious value and sets those who live it above their fellowman. In reality the only thing it does is repress, twist, warp, and stifle the wonderful life force God has given to us.

The strength of the positive approach: The positive approach is always the best approach. The positive suggestion is always the best suggestion. One day I was discussing this fact with a group of friends, and a lady in the group gave us a wonderful illustration of the effectiveness of a positive suggestion. She said when she was about fourteen, most of her girlfriends had acquired the habit of smoking. Because of this she too wanted to smoke and proceeded to ask her mother's opinion about the matter. Her mother didn't go into a rage and say, "Don't you dare smoke, I forbid it!" Instead she said, "Smoking isn't ladylike; you *do* want to be ladylike, don't you?" Now, I realize, and so does this fine lady, that many lovely ladies smoke, but I think this statement is a marvelous example of the positive approach.

When framing your suggestion for self-hypnosis always make it as positive as possible. I have dealt with some people who had to be beaten down with a negative suggestion, but they are few in number. The less conscious the effort involved in your self-hypnosis, and the more positive the suggestion, the greater will be your success.

PRINCIPLE 4
THE LAW OF ANTICIPATED JUDGMENT

One of the powerful forces in motivating men is that of anticipated judgement. This is perhaps one of the oldest tools of suggestion. "If you don't do right, you will be judged at the great judgment day." "Johnny, if you don't behave yourself, I am going to send you to the principal's office."

If you were to be told you had to improve something in your life within three weeks or suffer the consequences, I am sure you would make the improvement.

One of the oldest gimmicks for motivating people is the future promise. "If you work a little harder, I will give you a raise someday," etc. The individual who responds to this does so because he believes that sometime in the future he will be rewarded.

Most of us feel that someday and somewhere we have to give an account of our lives. In the use of self-hypnosis, it is a good idea to give yourself a deadline. You do not have to put this deadline in writing, but merely determine in your mind how long it will take you to accomplish your goal. In other words, give yourself a judgment day. You want to be more successful, but when do you want to be more successful: in six weeks, six months, or six years? When you give yourself a deadline, be realistic. Don't make it too soon because you will never reach it, and you will become discouraged and quit. Also, don't delay it too long, because your enthusiasm is likely to die.

Most of us work more consistently and constructively when we have a time schedule to meet; therefore, we should formulate a time structure for our self-hypnotic suggestions.

Another reason for a time element is that the subconscious is not aware of time in the ordinary sense of the word. It is very easy to distort time while under hypnosis. By a mere suggestion minutes can seem like hours or hours seem like minutes. Yet, on the other hand, the subconscious can be minutely accurate in regard to time. You can give the subconscious a command to awaken you at 5:33 A.M. and it will be more dependable than the best alarm clock made.

When you use self-hypnosis give yourself a definite, realistic deadline. If you reach the deadline without achieving the results you desire, make an evaluation and determine what has been accomplished. Then start again with a more realistic time schedule. I have found that three to six weeks is sufficient time to accomplish most goals. If your goal is a difficult one, you should at least begin to see some results within six weeks. The important factor is that the subconscious should be given a specific time structure by which to work.

PRINCIPLE 5
THE LAW OF ROLE PLAYING

Role playing can be a powerful force when combined with self-hypnosis. Dr. Jerome Frank, M.D., in his book, *Persuasion and Healing*, refers to certain experiments which give strong evidence that role participation on a strictly conscious level is capable of changing attitudes and producing conformity. If you pretend to believe something or act as though you are someone else, it will have some definite effect on your attitude and behavior. When a hypnotist has a very difficult subject to hypnotize, he uses what is known as the "role playing" technique. He tells the subject to act as though he is hypnotized whether or not he is. After a few weeks the subject usually is able to become hypnotized.

All of us have what psychologists call a "self-image." Your

self-image is the way you really see yourself in your mind. The self-image you perceive determines the role you play in life. If you visualize yourself as a failure, you play the role of a failure. If you visualize yourself as a success, you play the role of a success. However, it is possible to change your self-image by the proper use of your imagination and self-hypnosis. When you hypnotize yourself, see yourself as you desire to be, or visualize your goal as already accomplished. Before you get out of the bed in the morning, close your eyes and imagine yourself or your goal as a realized fact. Repeat the same process prior to retiring at night.

For instance, let us suppose your goal is self-confidence in a social situation. You read the suggestion you have written five times, then induce hypnosis. While under hypnosis visualize yourself as being confident when meeting people, while speaking publicly, etc.

If you imagine the goal and play the role, it won't be long until it will be realized.

PRINCIPLE 6
THE LAW OF REPEATED CONCENTRATED EXPOSURE

My concept of this law is three-fold. First, the more you are exposed to an idea the more it becomes a part of your thinking. When the right suggestion is repeated often enough it becomes highly effective. In fact, if any idea, be it true or false, is repeated often enough, it is usually believed by someone.

Another matter involved in this law is that the more your mind concentrates on an idea the more the idea becomes part of you.

The third aspect of this rule is that of exposure. Any time you are exposed to an idea, it has some effect on you. The effect might be negative or positive, but there is always an effect.

Think of the tremendous power of indirect exposure to an idea. You are being exposed to this type of suggestion every day of your life.

Emile Coue explained indirect exposure in this manner: He said that one idea begets another idea. For instance, let us imagine that you are not hungry. In fact, it has only been about an hour since you have eaten a very nice meal. But it is a hot, humid day, and you are taking a walk to the park. On the way to the park, you have to pass an ice cream stand. Now remember you are not hungry. Your appetite have been thoroughly satisfied. As you come near the ice cream stand you see the picture of a delicious ice cream cone. You see people standing around eating ice cream, and suddenly you become very hungry for it. Now, no one walks up and says, "Buy ice-cream." The sign bearing the picture of the ice cream cone doesn't say, "Buy ice-cream." But you buy ice cream because through the years you have been exposed to ice cream. The idea of ice cream produces the idea of pleasure. The sight of ice cream is an indirect suggestion which begets another suggestion.

Most of the suggestions to which you are exposed in your daily life are of this nature. Automobile manufacturers never display ads which say, "You buy our car." They merely show their automobiles in the most pleasing manner possible, hoping the pictures of beautiful cars will beget the idea in your mind of buying one. Repeated, concentrated exposure to an idea is very effective in producing a desired result, especially when used in hypnosis, because hypnosis is the ultimate in human concentration.

In order to illustrate the three facets of this law, imagine you have a huge log you wish to burn. You don't possess any matches but you do have a large magnifying glass. You could set this log in an open field and fully expose it to the rays of the sun for years, but it would never burn. But if you take your magnifying glass and hold it over the log, the heat of the sun's rays is concentrated and intensified so that combustion takes place. Since this is a large log, the process must be repeated a number of times before it is completely disintegrated. Now let us take the illustration a step further. Think of the log as being a behavior pattern which you want to change. You have exposed the behavior pattern to the "sun" of general good intentions for many years but it remains static. Then you take your general good intentions and allow them to shine through the "magnifying glass" of positive, concise suggestions, while under hypnosis. This causes combustion and burns away part of your behavior pattern. You repeat this process until the change you seek is effected.

I have already mentioned the fact that the results of hypnosis are temporary, but they are also cumulative. The first time you give yourself a suggestion the effects of the suggestion last for a few hours. The next suggestion stays with you a few more hours. Each time the duration is longer, until finally it becomes a habit pattern. When using a suggestion in conjunction with self-hypnosis, repeat the effort until you are successful.

HOW TO PUT THE PRINCIPLES TO WORK

Now notice how you can put these principles to work in writing your suggestions.

1) The first thing you must do, before applying any of the principles of this chapter, is to select a goal. Remember, your subconscious is a goal-striving mechanism. When deciding upon your goal be definite and specific in stating what you desire. Don't just say, "I want success." Tell your subconscious what kind of success—business success, athletic success, etc.

2) Give yourself a PDEM, and be as definite as possible. For example: "I want financial success in my business" (goal) "because I want to be financially independent at the age of 55." (PDEM). "When I study, my mind will absorb knowledge as a sponge absorbs water because I want a "B" average." "Because I want a "B" average" is both your goal and your PDEM.

3) Examine your suggestion to be sure it meets with your self-approval. If there are any inner conflicts, they must be resolved before you proceed further.

4) Apply the "law of reserve effect" and be sure your suggestion is framed in a positive manner. Also, be concise, because the less effort the better.

5) Give yourself a realistic time limit.

6) Visualize your new self-image as already being accomplished.

7) Repeatedly expose yourself to the suggestion by the use of self-hypnosis.

When writing your suggestion, take your time. Be concise and use simple, picturesque language. Write and rewrite your suggestion until you know it is the right one. It is difficult to explain how you know when a suggestion is the right one. I usually tell an individual that, if he can feel the emotional impact of the words, this is a good indication he has the right suggestion. This "knowing factor" is more emotional than intellectual. The inner mind seems to say, "This is it," whenever you choose the right words and phrases.

Once you have written a suggestion to your satisfaction, read it over and over, word by word, until you have almost memorized it. When you use it in conjunction with self-hypnosis read it to yourself or think it to yourself five to ten times before inducing self-hypnosis. After you have reached the condition of total, complete relaxation, let it float in your mind. Don't try to consciously think of it word for word at this point, but just let the idea float in your mind. The less conscious the effort the easier it will be reach the subconscious. Sometimes you can summarize your suggestion with a word or words which portray the idea to you. While you are in hypnosis allow this summary word to drift and float into your subconscious.

Remember when writing your suggestion to be concise, simple, and picturesque. When using your suggestion with self-hypnosis, read it repeatedly before inducing the trance, then allow the idea to drift and float in your mind. The less conscious effort you exert the better. Exercise your conscious efforts when framing the suggestion, not when you are using it.

HIGHLIGHTS TO REMEMBER FROM THIS CHAPTER:

1. The wording of a suggestion is just as important as the depth of the hypnotic trance.
2. It is, therefore, important that you understand the basics of suggestion.
3. The six principles of suggestion:
   (1) The law of the PDEM.
   (2) The law of self-approval.
   (3) The law of the reverse effect.
   (4) The law of the anticipated judgment.
   (5) The law of role-playing.
   (6) The law of repeated concentrated exposure.
4. How to apply these six principles in writing your suggestion:
5. When writing your suggestion give it much time and thought. Be concise and use picturesque language.
6. Read the suggestion over and over until you are thoroughly familiar with it.
7. Read or think it to yourself five to ten times before hypnotizing yourself. Then let it float in your mind.

10

HOW SELF-HYPNOSIS
CAN HELP YOU INCREASE
YOUR FAITH

WE BEGIN THIS SECTION WITH the subject of faith for a logical reason. It has already been brought to our attention that hypnosis is a "conviction phenomenon." When we substitute "faith" or "belief" for the word conviction we can begin to understand the importance of the subject of faith. The expression faith or belief, as used in this book, has no reference whatsoever to any particular religious faith or belief. The word faith means belief, confidence, credence, trust, or conviction.

Mr. Claude M. Bristol, in his book, *"The Magic of Believing,"* published by Prentice-Hall, Inc., draws attention to the fact that belief is the one common denominator of all miraculous phenomenon.

Did you ever stop to ask yourself if some of the unusual things you read and hear are true? Most people discount the miraculous by saying, "I don't believe it. It's a trick, etc." Yet there is proof positive that natives in the Pacific Islands walk on stones heated to 1600 degrees Fahrenheit. People in the hills of Kentucky have been bitten by poisonous snakes during religious services and suffered no ill fate. Cures have occurred at faith healing meetings and at religious shrines for which medical men have no rational explanation.

When you consider the part faith plays in all of these happenings, you will perhaps have to reevaluate the miracles recorded in Jewish and Christian Scriptures and other ancient writings. Consider and compare the native walking on hot stones, a man holding the lighted end of a cigarette against his flesh while self-hypnotized, the biblical account of the three Hebrew children walking in the fiery furnace. In all three instances they are exposed to tremendous heat which should do great harm. Yet none of them is harmed in any manner. What logical explanation can we give for this? Let's examine what takes place.

Before the native ventures to walk on the fiery coals, he receives a special blessing from his priest. He then walks on the hot stones to demonstrate his faith and the power of his deity. The self-hypnotized man holding the lighted end of a cigarette against his flesh has convinced himself that his flesh is anesthetized. He not only feels no pain, but he receives no blister. His belief is so effective that the subconscious responds in such a way to make him immune to pain and harm. Shadrach, Meshach, and Abednego believed Jehovah would deliver them from the burning furnace and He did. Conviction of belief is the one common factor in all three of these unusual happenings. All of these men had different objects of faith. The native has faith in his pagan priest and God. Jehovah was the object of faith for the Hebrews in the furnace. The man using self-hypnosis has belief in the science of hypnosis. Even though they have different objects of faith, all are successful.

FAITH AND BELIEF AS APPLIED IN THE MEDICAL FIELD

Faith and belief are also very important to the field of medicine. It is estimated by a number of competent physicians that seventy-five per cent of all illness is psychosomatic in nature. This means that three out of four sick people have psychosomatic illnesses. Psychosomatic is a word which means psych (mind) and soma (body). It refers to disease which is primarily caused by mental or emotional factors. Physicians speak of functional symptoms. A person suffering from a functional disorder will have certain physiological symptoms, but will be alright physically.

A PSYCHOSOMATIC CASE OF HEART ATTACK

A physician once sent a female patient to me who was having heart attacks that were not heart attacks. This seems rather confusing; let me explain. The lady was about forty-five years of age and was suffering from what seemed to be a heart disease. She had had four attacks during which she experienced violent chest pains, and on two occasions loss of consciousness. The physician hospitalized her and gave her every test possible, but all the tests proved her to be physically sound. Notice, this woman was physiologically experiencing shortness of breath, chest pain, and other symptoms of a heart attack. The subconscious mind had been convinced erroneously. It acted, nonetheless, producing certain reactions in the nervous system. These reactions were real to this lady.

After working with this woman for a short period of time, I was able to discover many reasons for her pseudo-heart attacks. She had done things in her past for which she believed she should be punished. It was a deep conviction in her subconscious mind that she should suffer and even die. She blamed herself for her mother's death. Her mother had died the previous year of a heart attack, and as a result, she was punishing herself with heart pains. Her subconscious was convinced she needed punishment and reacted according to this belief. You can think and talk yourself into sickness. The same things are true in getting well. Two of the most important things in recovering from an illness are the desire to get well and the belief that you will get well.

FAITH CAN ACCOMPLISH THE IMPOSSIBLE

Faith not only causes people to become ill and to get well, but faith can and has inspired men to accomplish the impossible.

Columbus certainly could not prove that the Americans existed, but he believed they existed. On the basis of that conviction he set out to discover the undiscovered. When an astronaut sets out on a journey, he knows where he is going. This is more than Columbus knew. Even though he might deny it, every man who has ever accomplished anything in life has been a man of faith.

Faith has built empires! Faith has blazed new trails! Faith has broadened horizons and given hope to multitudes! The United States is built on faith. In the early days of our country a man's word was his bond. If this trust had not existed our country couldn't have risen to such great heights. A friend of mine who is in the livestock business has transacted as much as $50,000 worth of business on the word of a Michigan farmer. We Americans, although we complain a lot, have great faith in our government. We have faith in our economy, our way of life, and our destiny. Above all, we have faith in one another. Think of the millions of dollars of credit that is granted every day by Americans to fellow Americans. A vivid example of our trust in each other is the fact that we not only use paper money backed by the government, but we also use paper checks, backed only by an individual's signature. In other words, an American's word is still, to a great extent, his bond.

All men have faith! Without it you could not function. The economic system of our nation would grind to a halt without faith. You have faith the sun will rise tomorrow, and you believe you will be alive in the morning. You also believe you will go to work tomorrow. Perhaps you never before thought of faith in these terms. Faith or belief do not have to be restricted to the mystical beliefs and creeds of religion.

Faith is a mechanism you are exercising every moment of your life: Faith in people, faith in a set of facts, faith in what you are doing and faith in yourself. Belief is involved in almost every activity of your life.

There are actually few things in this world about which you have complete knowledge. Partial knowledge is all you possess about most things. For instance, you have partial knowledge about the sun and earth. On the basis of this partial knowledge you believe the sun will rise in the morning. You believe it will rise, but you cannot prove it will rise.

THE LIMITATIONS OF PERSONAL KNOWLEDGE

Personal knowledge is another realm where we are limited. Most of the knowledge we possess is imparted knowledge. The only thing that can be called personal knowledge is that which we have personally seen, heard, or experienced. Yet there are many things we believe which we have not experienced. We believe Columbus discovered America, that two plus two are four, that the earth is round, and many other things, all because of imparted knowledge. In reference to personal knowledge, we believe because we have experienced. When we exercise faith in imparted knowledge we believe in the word of others. Belief is acceptance. You accept or take the word of another. When you exercise faith you give and you receive.

Once again, let me emphasize that faith or belief is a very important part of your being. You could not function without it! All normal men have faith!

EFFECTIVE FAITH STRENGTHENED BY HYPNOSIS

Belief is a tremendous force in our life. This is especially true when we add hypnosis or self-hypnosis to faith. When the subconscious mind is convinced, it begins to act. It is, therefore, imperative that we make sure the subconscious mind believes the right things. Let us begin by being certain we have the right kind of faith.

The right kind of faith will be a positive faith, a realistic faith, a limited faith, and an active faith.

The expression of your belief determines whether you have a positive faith or a negative faith. Unbelief is faith exercised in a negative manner.

A man with negative faith says, "I do not believe anyone or anything," or, "I do not trust him." He lives a life of distrust and unbelief. All his energies are expended to prove no one can be trusted. His whole life is a negation.

The man with positive faith says, "I trust him in regard to his occupation," or, "I trust him in financial matters." Everyone can be trusted in some way. This doesn't mean you are stupid or naive. It simply means you take the positive approach. You try to find the good in a man instead of the bad.

Have you ever noticed how willing some people are to find and exploit what they believe to be evil in others? If they hear something good about someone, they do not bother to repeat it, but if they hear an evil report, they cannot contain themselves until they have told many. They chew this gossip! They digest it! It is the joy of life for them to bathe themselves in the difficulties of others. These people invariably possess a negative faith. A negative faith will blight and destroy your life and the lives of those about you. It stifles progress and ambition. It kills and destroys good. All of the principles of righteousness are annihilated by negative faith, so rid yourself of it. With it you will never succeed. Avoid those who have it, and surround yourself with those who have positive faith.

A man who has positive faith will have positive thoughts and will possess positive character traits. This man can do only one thing—succeed. All the forces of God's Universe are at his disposal. Strive each day for this attribute, positive faith.

THE ELEMENTS OF A POSITIVE FAITH

If you are to have an effective, positive faith, you must have a realistic faith. A faith based on facts. Think of the ridiculous things some people believe. They entertain ideas for which they have absolutely no proof. Quite often, these baseless ideas twist and warp their lives, robbing them of happiness and forcing them to live lives of fear and anxiety.

It is amazing how men with a good degree of education cling to superstitious ideas which hinder and harm them. They possess some of the truths of the twentieth century, but they will not allow the truth to set them free. As absurd as it might seem, they are like Neanderthal men with college degrees. They are educated as to their work, but they do not know how to live.

A realistic faith is not a contradiction of positive faith. The one complements the other. Positive faith is your approach to a given situation. You look for the good. It is your desire to have a positive belief. Realistic faith directs you to what you can believe. For example, suppose you are an employer approached by a man looking for employment. In checking his references you find he was dismissed from a position three years ago. He was dismissed because a marital problem at home affected his work. Since then he has done quite well. He has a good recommendation from his last employer. If you exercise negative faith you will write him off. You will not hire him. If you have positive, realistic faith you will assess the facts and determine what you can believe about the man. On the basis of the evidence, you may believe the man's marital problems have been solved, and that he is capable of good work. Rationalism directs the approach of positive faith. When the two go together, they are indomitable. Your faith is always based on the best knowledge available to you. A positive faith without realism would be fatal.

Some people mistake folly for faith. They insult God by projecting their stupidity to Him. A man once told me he never had to buy gas. He said he had faith and because he had faith, God filled his gas tank so he could go to church. This might seem to be an extreme example, yet situations similar to this are enacted every day in this drama of life.

Since belief plays such an important part in our life, and since the subconscious uncritically accepts whatever is fed into it, let us be sure we are positive and realistic in our beliefs.

In order to have a positive realistic faith, we must learn to limit our faith according to the object of faith. We should not have the same degree of faith in a man as we do in God, nor is it intelligent to trust all men equally.

If you are a devoted believer in God, you trust your God implicitly and without reserve, but your faith in an individual is limited by what you know about him. The honest man, you trust as an honest man. The dishonest man, you trust as a dishonest man. This is another example of positive realistic faith and illustrates once again how all of these factors are interrelated.

One of the primary reasons why a great number of people get hurt is that they put the wrong kind of faith in the wrong people. To trust any human being completely is the height of folly. Not long ago, a young man sat in my office and sobbed out the story of his wife's infidelity. The man later had to spend some time in a mental institution to regain his emotional equilibrium. Before I go further let me state that I believe you should have confidence and trust in your mate. This trust, however, should be limited by the fact that we are all human. Humans can change. We are creatures of emotion. It is possible for us to hurt one another.

It is understandable that this young man should have experienced a good degree of shock when he discovered his wife's unfaithfulness. But because he had an unreserved, unrealistic, and unlimited faith in his wife, he became mentally and emotionally unbalanced. This is an example of immaturity in regard to belief.

As a small child, you have unlimited faith in your parents. This might also apply to other authority figures of your youth. If your parents tell you the moon is made of blue cheese you believe them. You trust them and their every word implicitly. During the maturing process, you begin to limit your faith in your parents. You still believe in them, you still trust and have faith in them, but it is a different type of faith. It is a limited faith. The realization that they are human and fallible, that they can and do make mistakes, limits your faith in your parents.

LIMITATIONS OF A REALISTIC FAITH

Notice, a realistic faith is self-limiting. It automatically limits itself according to the knowledge it has concerning the object of faith.

Some individuals never mature or learn to limit their trust in their parents. Even when they are forty or fifty years of age they look upon the opinion of their parents as being infallible. The word of such an individual's husband or wife means nothing. This is indeed a sad situation for the person affected in this manner, and it is even sadder for the marriage.

While others mature in regard to limiting their trust in their parents, they nonetheless feel the need to project unlimited trust on to someone else. In the case of the young man with the unfaithful wife, unlimited faith was projected on to the wife. This is a common situation in our country which stresses a neurotic type of love as a basis for marriage. The tragedy is that, after the neurosis weakens, the trouble begins.

Others project their unlimited faith to some other authority or parental figure. Many times it is a clergyman, a college professor, a political figure, a movie star, or some other personality.

Quite often, someone will come to me telling of how his heart has been broken by his minister. Invariably, I find that this person looks upon his minister not as a minister, not as a human being, not even as a man of God, but as God Himself. One day such a person becomes aware of the fact that his pastor is human, and as a human, is fallible. He is not actually hurt by the minister, but by his own erroneous faith.

Remember, you limit your faith according to the object of faith. Without this you cannot have a positive or realistic faith.

FAITH IN ACTION IS ESSENTIAL

Another important attribute your faith should possess is that of activity. You should have an action faith! Faith without works is dead! The only way you can prove your faith is by action.

Some of you might feel you would do more in your occupation, your home, your community, and your church if you had more faith. There are certain individuals you admire, and you respect them as men and women of great faith. If this is your case, I am now going to reveal something to you which can completely change your life. Hear the words of the Master: "If ye have faith as a grain of mustard seed, ye can say to yond mountain be thou removed, and it shall be moved."

Have you ever seen a mustard seed? It is not very large, is it? In fact, it is quite small. You can barely see it when you hold it in your palm. "Faith as a grain of mustard seed,"—not great faith or large faith, but actually tiny faith! Small faith with a potential for growth! The mustard seed when planted will grow into a large plant. The Lord Jesus was emphasizing the importance of using the faith you have. No matter how small your faith might be, it is capable of moving a mountain! Have you moved any mountains recently? Begin to use and exercise this mighty tool we call "faith." Start moving some mountains!

An arm or leg that is never used eventually withers and becomes useless. Faith that is not exercised in a positive way becomes useless. A seed that is never planted does not grow.

When faith is exercised, it begins to grow. As your faith grows, you are able not only to move a mountain, you can move mountains! You begin to realize: "All things are possible to him that believeth."

AN EXAMPLE OF FAITH IN ACTION

It is a wonderful experience to see faith germinate and grow. A young lady named Alice, who felt her life was ruined, came to me a few weeks ago. Her childhood had been hectic and insecure because of an alcoholic father and a bitter mother. A young man, who had promised her matrimony, had just jilted her. She felt completely rejected and hated the world. It was her feeling that you could trust no one. Life, to her, was nothing but emptiness and vanity.

I let her express herself and ventilate her hostilities, and then I reasoned with her, telling her that the depression, fear, and hostility existed because she had convinced her subconscious mind that the world was hateful. The subconscious mind, in return, unleashed these emotions back into her life. After a few counseling sessions Alice began to believe again. Her countenance showed a lovely smile and her whole demeanor changed. At her office her fellow employees noticed the difference, and her supervisor gave her a substantial raise because of the improvement in her work. What caused the change? Hypnosis and self-hypnosis were used to fill her subconscious mind with a positive, realistic, limited, active faith. She learned you can trust people, but you must trust them in a realistic, limited way. Today, Alice stands on her own two feet and is able to function effectively in her business and social world.

Alice's case was serious, but not as desperate as another situation with which I dealt. Alice knew something was wrong and sought help. Realizing your need and responding to it can mean everything when you have a problem.

EFFECTIVE FAITH HEALED AN ALCOHOLIC WIFE

A man with a problem came to see me a few years back. His problem was his wife; she was a total alcoholic. They had been married for 21 years and had four teenage children. She had been drunk, off and on, for the past five years. The oldest girl had assumed the role of mother and housekeeper. When this gentleman came home from work, his wife might be there or she might not. If she was home, she was probably inebriated. Her drinking had affected the children to such an extent that they had no respect for her. In fact, they wanted their father to divorce her. This is why he had come to see me. He had often contemplated divorce, but he still loved his wife and wanted her to be the mother and wife she used to be. Although he was seeking help for the situation, she wanted none. She felt that she was hopeless and refused to come.

After he had poured his heart out to me, I told him that deep down inside of her there was still a flickering of faith. If he wanted to salvage her, he must have faith for her. Notice, not merely faith in her, but faith for her. He couldn't quite comprehend what I meant, so I explained that, since she had no confidence in herself as a person, and no faith in her abilities it was up to him to believe for her. I wanted him to tell her he had been to see me and tell her what I had recommended. He didn't much believe it would work, but he said he would give it a try.

For the next two weeks he expressed his faith in her and demonstrated his faith for her. He treated her as if she weren't an alcoholic and helped her in every way possible. But when he came to my office he felt there was only slight improvement. We prayed together and asked God to give him the strength to continue. Finally, after six weeks his wife came to my office with him. She had been sober for six days and was now wanting help. To her, it seemed like someone had reached into the deepest recesses of her soul and formed new life and energy from the faith that resided there. Before long, she renewed her vows to her God and her church. Her life and home were restored because her husband loved her enough to have faith in her and for her.

Through all this, the husband also became a much better and stronger person. Whenever you have faith for someone else your faith becomes stronger.

A MASTER PROGRAM TO DEVELOP AND INCREASE FAITH

Let us now consider a constructive plan by which we can develop and increase the faith we have been discussing.

The word, faith, lends itself for a wonderful outline:

F   Forget past failure and think of past successes.
A   Actuate your faith.
I   Institute new goals. Give yourself a P.D.E.M. for faith.
T   Trust God and triumph over all obstacles.
H   Hope for a glorious future.

"F" means forget past failures and think of past successes. Thinking of all the bad and unfortunate things that have transpired in your life doesn't help anyone. All of us have experienced some difficult moments. Dwelling on these events accomplishes only one thing. It convinces our subconscious that all things have been difficult, and they will always be difficult. It will instill a very tenacious negative faith in our being. If, when thinking of the past, we will direct our thoughts to the happy, successful experiences we have had, we will develop a powerful positive faith. Unless we enjoy feeling sorry for ourselves and bathing in self-pity, we will find it just as easy to think of the good things as of the bad.

At the beginning it might take a little effort, but you can do it. It is a good idea not to think about the past too much, but when you do, think of the good things. The past is past. It can never be undone or brought back. You are living today, and it is important you live today to the fullest. Those who live in the past are merely existing; they are not living.

"A" means act upon your faith. Faith without works is dead. Have you ever noticed that many failures are people who have numerous ideas, but who have never done anything about them? If you have faith in an idea, do something about it. You believe your school needs a new library or your church needs a new building. Maybe you believe you need new furniture. Well, act upon this conviction. Put your faith to work. The average individual sits back and waits for someone else to do the job. Don't let this be you.

If you think it necessary that you increase your income, start to put your faith in action. You might be astounded at what will happen.

"I" means initiate new goals and move forward every day. Don't let life pass you by! Don't stagnate! The people who have really stayed alive until they passed into the after life have been people who have kept their minds alert. They have constantly sought new horizons and probed into new fields of endeavor. Churchill and Einstein are two well known examples of this truth, and there are many others.

"T" means to trust God and triumph over all obstacles.

"H" means hope for a good and glorious future. Hope is the forward aspect of faith. Modern science and technology are bringing forth a new and wonderful day in the history of man's existence. It will be wonderful unless it is misguided.

A man without hope is a man without a positive faith.
Your future can be what you hope it to be!
Put into practice these five things, and you will realize a positive faith in your life.

SELF-HYPNOSIS SUGGESTION TO INCREASE AND IMPROVE YOUR FAITH

Use the following suggestion, while in the state of self-hypnosis at least once a day for thirty days: Because I want (Insert your own P.D.E.M.) I always express a positive faith. This belief is limited by the object of faith. I always maintain an active, vigorous faith.

HIGHLIGHTS TO REMEMBER FROM THIS CHAPTER:

1. Since hypnosis is a "conviction phenomenon," faith and hypnosis are closely related.
2. The "belief phenomenon" is the one thing which explains most miraculous happenings.
3. Faith and belief play an important part in the field of medicine.
4. Faith has inspired men to accomplish the impossible.
5. The United States is built upon faith.
6. All men have faith; without it you couldn't function.
7. The right kind of faith is composed of four elements:
   (1) It is a positive faith.
   (2) It is a realistic faith.
   (3) It is limited by the object of faith.
   (4) It is an active faith.
8. Sometimes you must have faith for others.
9. A five point program for increasing and improving your faith is given.
10. A self-hypnosis suggestion is given for increasing your faith.

11

HOW SELF-HYPNOSIS
CAN INCREASE YOUR
SELF-CONFIDENCE

LACK OF CONFIDENCE IS THE most common of all psychological maladies. "I don't have any self-confidence," has become a general catchall phrase, which can be descriptive of something very trivial or of something of a more serious nature. The lack of self-confidence is the root of many difficulties. It can cause extreme distress and, in some situations, embarrassment to the person affected.

The individual who doesn't have confidence in himself will never be completely successful. Sometimes it will cause him to lose his position or keep him from advancing in his work. It might even keep him or her from being married! Warm genuine friendships will be denied the person who doesn't possess self-confidence. New experiences, adventure, and romance will bypass him on his journey through life. One thing is certain, the individual without confidence is going to miss out on many of the good things of life.

WHAT IS LACK OF SELF-CONFIDENCE?

Before we proceed further, we should explain what we mean by the expression, "lack of self-confidence." I have read numerous articles on this subject, but none have stated what lack of confidence is. The key to understanding self-confidence is to rephrase the expression. What are you actually saying when you say, "I don't have confidence in myself" or "I lack self-confidence"? To answer this question, replace the word 'confidence' with other words which mean basically the same thing but which will bring to your mind the impact of what you are saying: "I don't *trust myself.*" "I don't *have faith* in myself." "I *lack faith* in myself." When you say you don't have self-confidence, what you really mean is you don't trust yourself! You don't have faith in yourself! It is most important that you understand this because you can't competently deal with this problem unless you know what it is.

When you possess self-confidence you believe in yourself, you trust yourself, and you have faith in yourself. There are two general categories into which lack of self-confidence can be divided. An individual who almost completely lacks confidence in himself is usually said to have an inferiority complex. This type of person is almost totally without self-confidence. (Notice I said "almost totally," because no one is completely without self-confidence. The men and women who can be described as possessing self-confidence are people who are subconsciously convinced of their ability to cope with life. They believe they can fulfill whatever life demands of them. They possess the wonderful faculty of resiliency. They can roll with the punches, and get up when they are knocked down.)

The other general category of self-confidence, or the lack of it, is exemplified by the individual who seems to be basically confident, but who lacks confidence in certain segments of his life. Everyone has certain areas of his life in which he feels confident and certain areas where he lacks confidence. This varies from individual to individual. Some people possess confidence in most segments of their life. Others have very few segments of their lives in which they really feel confident. No one completely lacks self-confidence, and no one is completely self-confident. The man we term self-confident is basically confident in most aspects of his life, whereas the person with the inferiority complex lacks confidence in most areas of his life.

We all have certain areas in which we lack confidence and certain areas in which we possess confidence. You might be very confident in yourself as far as your work is concerned but be very unconfident in social situations. Perhaps it is easy for you to speak to one person, but you find it very difficult to address a group. You are confident on the ball field, but scared to death on the dance floor. The businessman may feel perfectly at home and self-assured in his office, but be ill at ease when in the presence of highly educated people. Mother feels secure and confident in her home, but when she has to mingle socially with her husband's business associates she falls apart. Junior has great confidence in sports, but has no faith in his ability to get good marks in school.

THE NATURE OF SELF-CONFIDENCE

Our last chapter was devoted to the subject of faith, and we pointed out what an important and vital part faith plays in your life. Some important guide-lines were also given in regard to the use of your faith. Now let us notice the five directions in which your faith is to be exercised. Your faith should go upward, inward, outward, forward, and backward. The upward aspect of your faith is your faith in God. The inward aspect of your faith is your faith in yourself. The outward aspect of your faith is your faith in your fellowman. The forward aspect of your faith is your faith in the future. The backward aspect of your faith is your faith in the past.

Another way of stating this, which will show you the relationship of all of this to the problem of self-confidence, is to change the word faith to confidence. The upward aspect of faith is divine confidence. The inward aspect of faith is self-confidence. The outward aspect of faith is what I call human-confidence or trust in your fellowman. The forward aspect of faith is future-confidence. The backward aspect of faith is historical- or traditional-confidence.

I have stated all of this for this reason; each aspect of "confidence" or "faith" is related to the whole. In other words, if you have a weak or unrealistic faith in God, you will have a weak, unrealistic confidence in yourself, in others, in the past, and in the future. Invariably, you will find that the man who lacks self-confidence usually lacks divine-confidence, human-confidence, past-confidence, and future-confidence. This might not be evident on the surface, but when you get down to the root of the problem you will find it to be true. For example, a savage who believes in a cruel god of retribution is usually cruel to himself and to his fellowmen and has little hope for the future. The person who believes in himself usually finds it easy to believe in God, his fellowmen, and the future.

An objection which might be raised by some is, how does this apply to the atheist? The answer to this is relatively simple. When the atheist says, "I don't believe in God," what he is really saying is, "I don't believe in the traditional orthodox concept of God." He believes in the deity of humanism. His belief in atheism becomes his deity. Quite often you will find an atheist who is more devoted to his "faith" than the average Christian. The fact still remains that each aspect of faith or confidence is related to the other four aspects. If the atheist has a strong belief in his "deity," he will have strong faith in himself, in others, and in the future.

I have met one or two men in my life who impressed me as genuinely believing in nothing. When I say, "nothing," I mean in God, themselves, mankind, the future, or the past. This once again proves my contention of the inter-relationship of faith.

Someone might object by saying, "I know people who have no confidence in themselves, but they have great faith in God and their fellowman." But do they, really? How do you know this for a fact? Maybe they have more self-confidence than they outwardly display. Or perhaps what you call a strong faith in God is in reality an abject fear of God.

HOW HYPNOSIS HELPED A YOUNG MAN
GET SELF-CONFIDENCE

It is amazing to me how people stumble over this simple truth concerning the nature of self-confidence. Lack of confidence in yourself is merely lack of faith in yourself. You don't trust yourself. Self-confidence is believing in yourself. Now that you know what it is you can begin to do something about it.

Not long ago I had a young man as a client who maintained that his lack of confidence was keeping him from advancement in his work and from marriage. He recited a long story of failure after failure, all caused by his never having the nerve to take advantage of the opportunities which came his way. Romance and marriage had bypassed him because he hadn't had the confidence to pursue the girls that appealed to him. After he related his tragic life history to me, I pointed out to him the meaning of lack of self-confidence, and how faith went in five directions, and how they were all related. He then asked me where he should begin? Should he begin trying to believe more in himself or in God, etc.? I recommended that he assess his faith to determine its weakest direction and begin to work on it. From there, he should proceed to work on the other aspects of his faith.

He decided that his faith in God was "in pretty bad shape." He started to attend church, a church of a different faith than mine, and developed a strong realistic divine confidence. In a very short period of time his confidence in himself grew by leaps and bounds. He was able to relate himself in a warm manner to others. Girl friends were no longer a problem to him—he had more girl friends than he had time or money to date. As always, I used hypnosis to impress these ideas into the subconscious, and I taught him the art of self-hypnosis.

BEGIN WITH WHAT HAS THE GREATEST APPEAL FOR YOU

Sometimes I tell people to begin to work on the strongest aspect of their faith or on all four aspects of their faith. It really doesn't make much difference, because when one segment of their faith is strengthened all the other segments are likewise strengthened. Begin at the place which has the greatest appeal for you. Believe that God is Love. Believe that He loves you. Believe that He loves the whole world of mankind. Believe that He has a glorious, wonderful future planned for you.

Many times the person who brags and boasts about his self-confidence is really very unsure of himself. An individual with real self-confidence is like a man who has real wealth. He doesn't have to go around displaying it because he is sure of himself; he believes in himself, and he isn't trying to prove anything to anyone. Usually the man who is the loudest, who brags the most, and who pushes the hardest has the deepest feeling of inferiority. He acts in this manner in an effort to cover up his feeling of inferiority and to give vent to his hostilities.

WHAT CAUSES ONE'S DISBELIEF IN HIMSELF?

What is it that causes an individual not to trust himself, not believe in himself? No normal person is born this way. A small baby has to trust himself. If he doesn't, he will never learn to crawl, walk, talk, or feed himself. Every normal person is born with confidence! People who lack self-confidence have been taught not to believe in themselves. They have been taught, "You are not as good as others." "You can't do it." "It can't be done." "Don't do it because you will be hurt." Perhaps these actual expressions were not used, but this is the impression conveyed to the impressionable young mind.

The parent who will not allow the child to learn to do things for himself is teaching the child lack of confidence. The child's parents do not believe in him; therefore, how can you expect him to believe in himself? An individual is born with faith, but this faith can either be weakened or strengthened. If the child's faith is to be strengthened, it must be nurtured and guided. He must be taught new pathways in self-confidence and trust. Often this takes time and effort on the part of the parent, for it is easier to do something for a child than to teach him how to do it himself. By this I do not mean you should make a three year old cook his own dinner or iron his own clothing. Teach your child self-reliance. Teach him to do things appropriate for his age. Show him how to stand on his own two feet. Help him to mature emotionally as well as physically. Keep a guiding hand on him, but don't squeeze too tightly. Let him learn how to think for himself. He will stumble once in a while—we all do! When he does, pick him up and once again point him in the right direction.

I have seen parents treat children in their late teens like babies in diapers. These people are neurotic and sick, and they are doing great harm to their children. A parent can do too much or too little for a child. But I believe that the child whom the parents neglect is better off, at least in the area of self-confidence, than the child with doting parents.

If you lack self-confidence, you lack it today, and you can't undo the past. What is written is written! What is done is done, and it is impossible to change the past. *But you can change the present and the future.* You can begin to believe in yourself. Can you give me one good reason why you shouldn't believe in yourself? The answer to this question is, "No." You might be able to give me some excuses, but you can't give me one legitimate reason why you shouldn't believe in yourself. Some of the most common excuses given by the unconfident are: "I have failed." "Nothing ever goes right for me." "I just can't get ahead." "I always feel nervous." "People don't like me." "I just don't have any ambition." "Everyone seems to be against me". This list of excuses could be an endless one, but remember they are excuses and not reasons.

POSITIVE STEPS TO ACQUIRE CONFIDENCE

Let me give you a number of reasons why you can and should believe in and trust yourself. Use these reasons as steps which will easily teach you the valuable but forgotten lesson of self-confidence.

First. You should believe in yourself because you were born with self-confidence. Yes, I know, you were also born helpless, but you were not afraid to do the things you could do, and you didn't worry about what you couldn't do. I believe that this example from babyhood gives us the clearest picture possible of what self-confidence is. It is something given to us by God. It is the heritage of our nature. It is our divine birthright.

Competency is not confidence. Competency can be a vital aid to increasing confidence, but it is not synonymous with self-confidence. I know and you know people who are very competent in their work and other areas of their life, yet they possess no confidence in their ability to do their work. These individuals often work under people who know far less than they know, but who have confidence in themselves and the little they do know. A young child is very incompetent. When he begins to walk, he quite often stumbles and falls, but he gets up again and again until he is finally able to walk and run. His self-confidence is not evidenced by his competency, but by the fact that he keeps getting up every time he stumbles or falls. God help us to relearn this lesson and to unlearn the destructive lessons taught to us by our well meaning peers.

The young child also doesn't worry about what he can't do. Self-confidence is not competency nor is it conquering. By the word "conquering" I mean that you will never be able to do everything, for life is too short. Also, there will have to be certain things done for you that you won't be able to do for yourself. I can't place a three hundred pound weight over my head. I can't run the mile in four minutes. I can't read three thousand words per minute. I can't quote all of Shakespeare from memory. I am not as handsome as Rock Hudson. I don't earn five thousand dollars per week. And I don't own a million dollars. I send my suits out to be cleaned. I go to a dentist for the care of my teeth. I go to a physician for the care of my body. And I take my automobile to a mechanic when it needs repairing. But none of this bothers me. I don't even envy the people who do the things I can't do. And it doesn't embarrass me to have people do things for me which I can't do for myself. Yet I consider myself a confident person because I believe in myself.

Some things I don't do well, but I don't lose sleep over it. I believe that whatever I undertake to do, I can do it. The other fellow might do it better than I, but I will do my best. This is the important thing. "A little child shall lead them." You were born with self-confidence. Competency is not self-confidence. Self-confidence envies not; neither does it fret.

Second. You should believe in yourself because God loves you and believes in you. The very fact the Creator allows you to exist demonstrates that He loves you and believes in you. A few will object to these statements, and it is their right as free souls to do so. But to my simple mind these are self-evident facts. God believes in you enough to allow you to live and serve in His world. There is a divine purpose in your existence, and it is important that you discover that purpose. It just makes good sense to believe in yourself if God believes in you. He knows all your weaknesses and faults, yet still He has confidence in you.

Third. You should believe in yourself because others believe in you. Some might be inclined to disagree with this, but it is true. No matter how many times you have failed and fallen short of your goals, there is someone who believes in you.

A man came to see me and told me of his many "flops in life." I told him there was still someone in the world who believed in him, and he told me I was crazy. He said his wife didn't have enough confidence in him to send him to the store to buy a loaf of bread. All of their savings had been lost in a recent business venture, which had caused a backwash of family and financial troubles. I asked the gentleman if he had children, and he told me they had two boys and a baby girl.

To prove my point to him, I had him call in his ten year old son, who had been waiting for him. I asked the boy what kind of a person his father was, and he told me he was the greatest. Next, I asked him if he believed in his father, if he believed in his word, if he believed in his ability to succeed in business, etc. The young fellow told me he believed his father could do anything he wanted to do. He knew dad had had some tough breaks, but he still believed his dad could make it.

There is someone in this world who believes in you. In fact, most of you have many who believe in you: your wife, children, the kid down the street, your boss . . . Don't let them down by not believing in yourself.

Fourth. You should believe in yourself because, unless you do, many of your talents will never be realized and your goals will be unfulfilled. The average person is almost totally unaware of the talents and gifts which are his. He is afraid to try; he is afraid to adventure; therefore, they are never discovered. If he is aware of them, he is afraid to develop them. I have known a number of men and women who maintained they couldn't speak to a group when asked to teach a Sunday School class. But when they increased their divine confidence they developed some self-confidence and started to teach. To say they were amazed is to put it lightly. They were astounded. Talents which had been latent for years came to life.

An engineer, who had studied to be a painter, came to me one day and told me how miserable he was because he had not pursued the career of art. Shortly after finishing art school he had married and had to seek gainful employment. Through the years he continued with his painting as a sideline. But he felt he had missed his mark in life because he couldn't devote his full time to his first love. He was in a position financially where he could quit the engineering job and paint full-time, provided he could earn a fair sum from his art work. I know very little about art, but a number of this painter's friends told him that his work was good, and it would sell. The problem was that he had never displayed his paintings where it would count because he was afraid they wouldn't measure up. This man was denying himself the fulfillment of his life, not because he couldn't paint, but because he wouldn't believe in himself.

Fifth. You should believe in yourself, because you owe it to yourself to do so. It will develop your personality and shatter your egotism and self-centeredness. I say this kindly, yet truly. A person who lacks self-confidence possesses a large amount of self-consciousness. Self-consciousness is the enemy of self-confidence. An individual who lacks confidence is thinking too much about himself and too much about what others are thinking about him.

Perhaps some of you can remember the first time you ate in a sophisticated restaurant. You were scared to death! "How do I look? Am I walking right? Did I do that correctly? Oh, I don't want to spill any food or drop the silverware. Am I using the right fork? Why is everyone looking at me? . . ." You were so miserable thinking about yourself and the opinions of others that you didn't enjoy the food or the occasion. Today, you could go into that same restaurant and think nothing of it. You would sit down, relax, and enjoy it.

The person who is always overly concerned about what others are thinking about him is really flattering himself, because most people aren't noticing him. They couldn't care less about how he walks, talks, or how he holds his fork. The sooner he realizes this, the happier and wiser he will be. People will like you, not because of your manners and dress, but because you are genuinely you. By this statement, I don't mean you should disregard good manners and dress, but I am stressing the importance of relaxing and being your real self. Good manners are natural manners. Likeable people are natural people. Self-confident people are natural people. When you start believing in yourself, you will stop thinking about yourself.

You owe it to yourself to believe in yourself, because if you don't, others won't. Employers, employees, clients, etc. simply won't have confidence in you. I have already pointed out that someone always believes in you, but if you won't believe in yourself the vast majority of people will not believe in you.

I am quite often asked the question, "Do you believe a person can become over-confident?" First, let me state that I do not think you can believe too much in yourself. That is, you cannot believe too much in your God-given talents, abilities, in your worth, or in your potential. In order to properly use self-confidence, you must apply the four principles of faith to your faith in yourself. Your approach should be positive. You should approach yourself with a believing attitude. Your assessment or evaluation of yourself should be realistic.

Of course, you should limit your efforts or endeavors according to the abilities and talents God has given you. Everyone can't be good at everything, but this mustn't keep you from having confidence in yourself. You must also limit your endeavors according to your training. A man who has had no training in medicine or surgery shouldn't attempt to perform surgery just because he has confidence in himself. I wouldn't let him operate on me! Likewise, I wouldn't want a trained surgeon to operate on my body if he didn't have confidence in himself as a surgeon.

The last principle of faith to be applied is that of action. What you can do, do. Put your abilities, your talents, and your training to work. If you lack self-confidence your capabilities are wasting and rusting because of idleness.

If you will apply these four guide-lines to your faith in yourself, you can't help but achieve self-confidence which will be meaningful and lasting.

A PROGRAM TO INCREASE SELF-CONFIDENCE WITH SELF-HYPNOSIS

I am going to give you a step-by-step program which will enable you to increase your self-confidence with the aid of self-hypnosis.

1. As much as possible, determine the nature of your problem. Do you possess an inferiority complex—almost complete lack of faith in yourself? Or do you lack confidence in some particular segment of your life such as in work, social situations, the opposite sex, etc.?

2. When you have made this determination, give yourself a definite goal of achieving your need. If you feel you have an in-

feriority complex, your goal should be that of general increased faith in yourself. It might be wise to include greater faith in God and in others as a part of your goal.

If you lack confidence in a specific area, be sure to designate it in your goal. For example, "I want increased confidence when playing golf."

3. Apply all six of the principles of suggestion when writing your suggestion. Be certain to give yourself a strong P.D.E.M. "I am going to believe in myself because I want—romance—increased wages—success in my work." Be very specific with your P.D.E.M. as: "I am going to have more confidence when playing golf, because I want to be superior to George Jones . . . !"

4. Hypnotize yourself at least once a day until you achieve your goal.

5. Use self-hypnosis and your imagination to change your self-image. See yourself as self-confident. Visualize yourself acting confidently in various life-situations.

6. Let your mind dwell on things in which you are confident. Tell yourself you can do anything which is necessary for your happiness and well-being.

7. Begin to trust in yourself more and more each day. Give yourself the benefit of the doubt.

8. Begin to increase your faith in God and others. Read inspirational literature. Remember, your attitude toward God and others determines to a great extent your attitude toward yourself.

9. Stop thinking about yourself and what others think about you. Learn to laugh at yourself.

10. Don't be afraid to take a chance. Don't be afraid to make a mistake.

SELF-HYPNOSIS SUGGESTIONS FOR INCREASING YOUR SELF-CONFIDENCE

1. I will believe in myself because of (insert your own P.D.E.M.) And because I was meant to be self-confident. Because God believes in me. Because others believe in me. Because I will be able to develop latent talents and abilities. Because I owe it to myself.

2. I will have confidence in my (insert your own goal) because of (insert your own P.D.E.M.).

HIGHLIGHTS TO REMEMBER FROM THIS CHAPTER:

1. Lack of self-confidence can deny you many of the good things in life.
2. Lack of self-confidence means you lack faith or trust in yourself. You don't believe in yourself.
3. There are two general categories in regard to lack of self-confidence. (1) An almost complete lack of faith in yourself. This is commonly called an inferiority complex. (2) Lack of self-confidence in certain aspects of your life.
4. Faith or confidence moves in five directions.
   (1) Upward—divine-confidence
   (2) Inward—self-confidence
   (3) Outward—human-confidence
   (4) Forward—future-confidence
   (5) Backward—historical-confidence
5. Each aspect of faith is related to the whole.
6. Quite often the boasting, bragging person acts this way to cover up his real feeling of inferiority.
7. People who don't trust themselves were taught not to trust themselves.
8. There are five reasons why you should believe in yourself.
   (1) You were born with confidence.
   (2) God believes in you.
   (3) Others believe in you.
   (4) Hidden, dormant talents and abilities will be realized.
   (5) You owe it to yourself.
9. Self-consciousness is the enemy of self-confidence.
10. Apply the four principles of faith found in Chapter 10 to your faith in yourself.
11. A ten point program for achieving self-confidence with self-hypnosis is given.
12. Two sample self-hypnosis suggestions are given for increasing self-confidence.

12

HOW SELF-HYPNOSIS
CAN IMPROVE YOUR
HUMAN RELATIONSHIPS

ANOTHER TITLE WE COULD HAVE used for this chapter would have been: "How Self-Hypnosis Can Increase Your Human-Confidence." When your faith in your fellowman is increased, your relationship with him is automatically improved.

Most of the trouble and confusion that exists in the world is because man is incapable of getting along with man. Whence cometh arguments, violence, murder, divorces, wars, strikes, and lockouts? They come from man's inability to be at peace with himself and others. One of the biggest problems of any organization is "keeping the peace." Every small office and every major corporation is confronted with this problem.

The smart employer considers two factors when hiring someone for a position: his ability to do his work and his ability to get along with others. An individual who causes friction and strife in his work environment is never considered a desirable employee. He might be very productive, but the friction he produces off-sets his productions. If he agitates ten other employees to such an extent that their production is lowered, his own ability means very little.

THE IMPORTANCE OF GETTING ON WITH PEOPLE

One of the greatest abilities you can possess is sociability! The ability to get along with people is the greatest asset you can possess. If you own this priceless commodity, you will have a happy marriage, many loyal friends, sufficient income, and complete fulfillment in life. No man is an island. No man lives to himself. We all cross each other's path. Human engineering is the greatest challenge of this generation. If we are to have peace in the home, in the community, in the nation, and in the world, we must learn how to get along with each other. Man has learned how to conquer many things, but he has not learned how to conquer his own nature.

As a pastor, I have had to learn how to get along effectively with people. At times I have tried letting others have their way most of the time. This method kept the peace, but it was rather deadly to the ego. When this approach was used, I degenerated to the level of a "yes man." Usually I was the errand boy of inferior people with little ideas.

Another technique I tried was overpowering people. With the use of pressure and coercion I would win the issue, but lose the goodwill of the people. Neither of these approaches are constructive or effective.

THE "REALITY ACCEPTANCE FORMULA"

After many years of pastoral counseling, I developed an approach to my fellowman which I have found to be fruitful and satisfying. I have summarized it into what I call my "Reality Acceptance Formula" which is explained below.

1. I will accept myself as I am.
2. I will accept others as they are.
3. I will accept life as it is.

If you can master this formula as it is given in this chapter, you will have no difficulty in mastering yourself, others, or life.

ACCEPT YOURSELF AS YOU ARE

If you want to better your relationship with your fellowman, you must first learn how to get along with yourself. Your attitude toward yourself determines your attitude toward others. In our last chapter we set forth the fact that if you won't trust yourself you won't trust others. Now we will carry this truth even further. Jesus said that the second great commandment was to "Love thy neighbour as thyself." Someone has aptly mentioned the fact that the most important word in the statement was the word "as." If you cannot love yourself, you will find it impossible to love others. If you find no peace within yourself, it will be difficult for you to be at peace with your neighbor. If you cannot respect yourself, you will be unable to have a genuine respect for your fellowman. The man who hates the world really hates himself. The man who is always angry with others is really angry with himself.

When Jesus told us to love our neighbor as we love ourselves, He wasn't referring to an egocentric sick type of self-love. He was teaching us to have a healthy attitude of respect and compassion toward ourselves. He wanted us to view ourselves as being in the image of our creator, as being of great worth in the eyes of God. I think anyone who studies His teachings in depth will come to this conclusion. It will be natural for the person who loves and respects himself, who trusts himself, who views himself as being of great worth, to have this same attitude toward others.

Unfortunately, not everyone loves himself in this manner. There are innumerable people who lack this self-attitude, but it is possible for these people to acquire the self-love described by Christ. The first step in doing this is to accept yourself as you are. This is not meant to be taken as fatalism. It simply means that, perhaps for the first time in your life, you stop and take an honest look at yourself. You may like or dislike what you see. The important thing is that you stop fooling yourself. You can't correct a weakness in your life unless you first acknowledge the weakness to yourself.

When you accept yourself as you are, you begin to correct that which can be corrected, and you accept that which cannot be corrected. Most things which you consider a weakness can be changed. There will be, however, some things which you consider undesirable that cannot be remedied. For instance, you might feel you are too short or too tall. These fiats of nature cannot be altered. You can compensate for them to some extent by your dress and posture, but you can't change them. The best thing you can do is develop the right attitude toward your height. "I am short, but so what, a lot of great men have been short . . ." "I am extra tall; therefore, I will be proud of my height. I might even become a professional basketball player. . . ."

You can't change a withered limb, but you can change a withered spirit. Maybe you can't change a bad back, but you can change a blind mind. You can't change a bad heart, but you can change an evil heart.

Guide-Lines for an inventory of yourself: Take an honest inventory of your life and see what needs correcting. I will just mention a few guide-lines, but I am sure there are many other items you will be able to add.

1. Am I overly jealous?
2. Do I have too much temper?
3. Is my tongue too sharp?
4. Do I have real concern for others?
5. Am I distrustful of others?
6. Do I lack self-confidence?
7. Do I lack healthy self-love?
8. Am I too self-centered?
9. Do I have real faith?
10. Am I filled with anxiety?
11. Do I nag too much?
12. Am I really interested in my work?
13. Do I give my employer an honest day's work?
14. Do I harbor unnecessary guilt feelings?
15. Do I hate myself?
16. Am I pursuing a path of self-destruction?
17. Am I drinking too much?
18. Am I over-eating?
19. Do I get enough exercise?

20. Am I growing spiritually and intellectually?
21. Am I taking my wife or husband for granted?
22. Do I spend enough time with my children?
23. Is my ambition fading?
24. Am I at a standstill in my life and career?
25. Am I afraid of people?
26. Do I feel sorry for myself?
27. Do I read enough?
28. Am I a self-starter?
29. Have I accepted failure as my lot in life?
30. Do I have a friendly attitude?
31. Do I really have an unlimited faith in God?

All of the things mentioned on this check list can be corrected, if you have the desire to do so. Remember, your attitude toward yourself determines your attitude toward others.

Les Giblin, in his wonderful book *How You Can Have Confidence And Power In Dealing With People* (published by Prentice-Hall Inc.,) points out a fact which blends beautifully with this line of thought. He says that a man with an undernourished ego can think of no one but himself. He cannot, therefore, relate effectively with others. A man who is hungry can think of nothing but food and the satisfaction of his starving appetite. Likewise a man who lacks confidence, love, and respect for himself thinks of nothing but himself and the satisfaction of his starving appetite.

Accept yourself as you are, then change yourself into what you want to be. At the same time, reconcile yourself to what cannot be changed.

ACCEPT OTHERS AS THEY ARE

You will never be successful in dealing with your fellowman until you learn to accept him as he is. To accept someone as he is doesn't necessarily mean you approve of what he does. One of the major problems in the world today is that everyone is trying to get everyone else to conform to their ideas and their way of life.

You will never gain the friendship of anyone unless you do accept him as he is. How far would a counselor get with dope-addicts or homosexuals if he didn't accept them as they are? If he immediately begins to preach at them and condemn them, he will never see them again. These are people with severe problems, who are looking for someone who will treat them as a part of the human race. If the therapist displays a "holier than thou art" attitude, he loses the war before the battle begins. He must accept his patients as being the creation of God, as individuals of great potential worth, and as people worthy of respect.

On the other hand, if he were to act as though they had no problems, he couldn't help them. This is why I call my formula "The Reality Acceptance Formula."

Now let us take this clinical philosophy and project it into some of your life situations. Would you like to have a broader range of friends? Then begin putting this formula into practice. Would you like to be more effective in helping others? Then stop condemning them and start accepting them! Do you want to improve your human relationships in your factory or office? Then start to use this formula which can't help but work, if you will use it.

The Golden Rule: A short while back, I had a salesman as a client, who was constantly going backwards. He had taken over a new territory and was losing more customers than he was gaining. He came to me to find out why. Well, it didn't take long to find out why. I don't believe I have ever met a more opinionated person in all my life. When he went into a customer's office, he would proceed to try to change all of the customer's political, religious, and social beliefs. He might even tell him to change the office furniture or the color of the paint on the wall. Then he would try to sell an order. You can imagine how effective he was at this stage of the game.

Not many of you are this adamant and aggressive with your ideas, but perhaps you have some tendencies in this direction. Most people do. To overcome this detrimental habit, begin to treat the other person as you would have him treat you. Respect his beliefs and customs even as you would have him respect your beliefs and customs. I have a large number of friends with whom I differ on many points. We are well aware of the fact we disagree. At times we discuss our differences, but always with mutual respect.

The reason why the Apostle Paul was so successful in spreading the Christian Gospel was because he was "all things to all men" (I Cor. 9:22). He didn't criticize the Gentile and his culture or the Hebrew and his religion when he first met them—he accepted them as they were. Jesus Christ said, "I have not come to condemn the world . . ." (John 3:17 K.J.V.). He was the friend of publicans and sinners. He accepted people as they were. I am sure that neither of these men approved of everything these people did, but this didn't stop them from accepting them.

After you have accepted someone as he is, and he has accepted you as you are, find something you can praise in him. There is always something in everyone which will meet with your approval. Some of the nicest people I have ever met, on a professional basis, have been people with extreme behavior patterns. These individuals have been rejected by "decent society." Yet despite their "abnormalities" they are some of the finest people I have ever had the pleasure to meet. Because of my encounter with them, I feel that my life has been greatly enriched. I haven't as yet adopted any of their habits, but I have acquired greater understanding and compassion.

Giving praise costs you nothing, and yet it can win you many valuable friends. It can increase your income. It might even save your marriage or your position at work! The person who is unsure of himself or at war with himself will find it difficult to praise or approve of someone else. His "ego bank" is so short on funds it doesn't have any praise to spare.

After you have accepted an individual as he is and have found something in him of which you can honestly approve, begin to accentuate the things which you have in common. You will be surprised by the large number of mutual interests you have with the individual you consider to be completely different from you. Sports, music, art, drama, religion, and politics are just a few of the interests which may be held in common with others.

It would be difficult, if not impossible, for you to come into contact with someone who couldn't agree with you on some subject. Start cultivating the habit of being agreeable. It is very easy to get into a critical argumentative rut. You no doubt know someone who will argue about everything and anything. This type of personality doesn't help one to win friends and influence people. In fact a person of this type will have a difficult time in keeping what few friends he has.

Best ways of dealing with people: When dealing with people, especially the first time, do not emphasize your differences. Instead, accentuate the positive. Maybe an individual will differ with you in the realm of politics. He belongs to a political party which professes viewpoints completely divergent from your own political ideas. Yet, even so, you can find something in this area on which the two of you can agree. If your political beliefs are different concerning domestic issues, they may be similar in regard to foreign policy. If this is true, stay away from the domestic issues and keep the conversation on the foreign issues. Accentuate the positive so that your friendship may have an opportunity to grow and increase.

You probably have noticed I am using the letter "A" in outlining your approach to your fellowman: Accept, Approve, Accentuate. Now the final step is to advance your ideas and thoughts. This last point will, of course, only apply to those who have ideas and thoughts they wish to advance. If your purpose is merely to create friendships and advance goodwill, you won't need to practice this last point. But for those who must sell products or ideas, never forget this little "4A" formula: Accept people as they are, approve of something they do, accentuate your common interest, and, finally, advance your ideas. This whole process can take place in five minutes or it might take five years, depending on the person and the circumstances.

Now that I have given you what might be termed the positive approach in accepting others as they are, let me point out some pitfalls you should avoid.

One: Avoid pettiness. Petty people are immature people. It is impossible for them to get ahead because they are too busy "getting back."

Such a person might win some petty victory, but he will lose the love, friendship, and respect of many people. Little men never become great men. Settling the score doesn't always win the game. Wounding someone else doesn't heal your wound. A negative attitude, a bitter spirit, and a hostile nature are all the result of pettiness. Avoid pettiness as you would avoid the plague.

Two: Avoid prying. No one cares for anyone very long who is constantly asking personal questions. People will usually tell you what they want you to know. If they do not volunteer certain information, it is because they feel it is none of your business. If you want to create distrust, and have a huge question mark placed on your motives, just ask too many questions. Individuals who do not exceed the bounds of good taste in this area are the recipients of trust and confidence.

Three: Avoid prejudice. When I use the word prejudice, I am using it in its broadest sense. Do not close your mind to certain people, traditions, ideas, and cultures without first accepting them and evaluating them in a positive manner. Blind prejudice will rob you of enriching friendships and experiences. It dwarfs the mind and drowns the spirit.

Four. Avoid picking. Everyone has faults, but no one appreciates someone who is forever pointing them out. Remember everyone, and that includes you, has faults. Naggers and needlers are never on top of the social list. They might be on some other kind of list, but not the social list.

Five. Avoid pride. By pride, I mean vain pride. It is never wrong to have pride in your appearance, pride in your work, pride in your family, but don't be so proud that you can't take a joke. Learn to laugh at yourself. Don't carry a chip on your shoulder. Someone will knock it off. Most people with excessive pride actually have very little of which they can be proud.

These are just a few of the things you should avoid if you want to win friends and influence people. I am certain you can add many other items to this list. It might be a good idea to jot some of them down right now before you forget.

ACCEPT LIFE AS IT IS

Be realistic about life and at the same time be optimistic. These two attitudes walk together in beautiful harmony. There is no contradiction between them. Instead, they complement one another. You cannot have genuine optimism unless it is secured on a foundation of realism. What sometimes passes for optimism could be better described as delusion.

If you accept yourself as you are and others as they are, you will find it easy to accept life as it is. You accept life for better or for worse. No matter which it is, you intend to live it and improve it. Life can be enjoyed no matter what the circumstances are. Your attitude is the all-important thing which determines whether or not you enjoy life. The Apostle Paul and Silas sang praises to God in a jail house at the midnight hour, despite the fact that they had bleeding backs and bruised muscles. Men could beat their bodies, but they couldn't change their attitude.

A realistic attitude is fundamental: When you have a realistic, optimistic attitude toward life, you have a better chance of achieving success and happiness. Be realistic, don't expect something for nothing. You get out of life what you put into it. We live in an age that has a "What I can get from it or what will it do for me" attitude. Only a few think in terms of what they can contribute to life. People enter into positions, into marriage, and even into church membership with the idea of receiving but not giving. You reap from life what you sow.

I recently talked with a young college graduate who was very disturbed. He had just graduated, and no one had offered him the pay and position he expected. Good pay and wonderful opportunity had been offered, but no one had proposed to make him a vice president and start him at $25,000 per year. This young man had seen too many Hollywood movies and read too many success articles. He failed to realize that you start at the bottom and climb to the top.

Be realistic, don't expect everyone to like you all of the time. Everyone has his or her enemies. This doesn't bother me because I feel sorry for those who don't have the good sense to like me. Be yourself. Be friendly. Like everyone. Still there will be individuals who will be hostile toward you. These people will dislike you no matter what you do. There is nothing you can do to placate them. The best thing you can do is to adopt my humble attitude of feeling sorry for these poor misguided souls.

Be realistic, don't expect to have everything go your way all the time. There is no need to expect it because it won't happen.

I remember that when, as children, we played baseball, one boy would furnish the bat and another boy would furnish the ball. If something happened that one of them didn't like, he would take his bat or ball and go home. The other boys soon grew tired of this, and brought their own balls and bats. As a result, those two boys were left out of the game.

The game of life is very similar to this. Those who can't learn to play the game according to the rules of life are sometimes left out of the game. There is no one so important that he can't be replaced in the game of life. Babies usually get their way, but adults must learn to give and take.

Be realistic, don't look for perfection in anyone or anything. Instead of looking for perfection in life, begin to enjoy life. Learn to enjoy the little things in life. Appreciate nature. Be thankful and develop a pleasurable attitude toward the so-called bad things in life. The next time it rains become a child once again— go out and get yourself soaking wet! Your neighbors will think you have gone crazy, but it will do something for you. Go down to an old fashioned Coney Island and buy yourself a hot dog. Enjoy the little things in life once again.

SELF-HYPNOSIS SUGGESTION FOR IMPROVING YOUR HUMAN RELATIONSHIPS

Because (Insert your own P.D.E.M.) I will accept myself as I am, others as they are, and life as it is.

HIGHLIGHTS TO REMEMBER FROM THIS CHAPTER:

1. Most of the trouble in the world today stems from man's inability to get along with his fellowman.
2. One of the greatest abilities you can possess is sociability.
3. Accept yourself as you are.
   (1) Your attitude toward yourself determines your attitude toward others.
   (2) Accept what you can't change.
   (3) Correct what needs to be corrected.
4. Accept others as they are.
   (1) A therapist must learn to accept others as they are if he is to help them.
   (2) Learn to respect the beliefs and ideas of others.

(3) Find something of which you can approve.

(4) Accentuate your common interests.

(5) Advance your ideas.

(6) Avoid these five things: Pettiness, prying, prejudice, picking, pride.

5. Accept life as it is.

(1) Don't expect something for nothing.

(2) Don't expect everyone to like you all the time.

(3) Don't expect everything to go your way all the time.

(4) Don't expect perfection in anyone or anything.

6. A self-hypnosis suggestion is given for improving your human relations.

13

HOW SELF-HYPNOSIS
CAN HELP YOU LIVE
WITH THE PAST

TOMORROW, TODAY WILL BE YESTERDAY. Just as man cannot live without a relationship to his fellowman, even so he cannot sever himself from the past. We all have two pasts: our personal past and the historic past of man. The first one is of our making, but we had nothing to do with the second. The historic past was ready made for us when were born. Even though we played no part in its creation, it still has a tremendous effect upon our lives. It determines our social status, our economic potential, our religious beliefs and our cultural attitudes. Though we have nothing to do with the formation of our own past, we are at this very moment producing a past for coming generations.

WHAT TO DO WITH OUR PAST

What are we to do with our historic past? How are we to live with the traditions that have been bestowed upon us by our fathers? There are three general attitudes toward the past, as follows:

1. *Deny, destroy, and forget the traditions of the past.* Anything from the past is reactionary and of no value; therefore do away

with it and begin anew. Leave "the faith of our fathers" with our fathers, we don't need it. This is the philosophy of those who have no faith in the past.

This attitude is evidenced in many ways, including the destruction of historic buildings and landmarks in many of our major cities and the emphasis placed upon youth. I am for the youth of our nation, but I am also for the older citizens. They have made, and still can make, a vital contribution to our society.

2. *Live in the past.* Allow the traditions which might have been practical and sensible five hundred, a thousand, or two thousand years ago to influence your life. Perhaps these same traditions are without any value or meaning today, but if they are old, they must be good. Or so say those who want to live according to the traditions of the past.

Old wine is good and of great value, but old meat is rotten and poisonous. Some traditions are good and some are bad. The world is slow in making progress because people and nations want to cling to ideas and practices which hinder the evolution of social improvement. "What was good enough for daddy is good enough for me." "Give me the good old days." I seriously doubt that those who make these statements really want to go back to the good old days and live as dad lived.

Modern civilization has its faults, but the average man is living better today than ever before. We have better food, clothing, housing, education, communication, transportation, sanitation . . . No other era of history can even begin to compare with this modern age. Apart from these material advantages, man is more tolerant and experiences a greater degree of personal freedom.

If you want to bring back the good old days, how far back do you want to go, and how much do you want to bring back? By the good old days do you mean the Roaring Twenties or the Victorian Age or the time of the Puritans or the Medieval Era or the time of Christ? Do you want to bring back the slavery, disease, and human degradation which existed during various periods of man's history?

No, it is not good or sensible to live in the past. You are living today; therefore, get in step with the age.

3. *Blend the good of the old with the good of the new.* Build upon the enduring rational traditions of the past. This will build a strong traditional confidence. A tree that has no roots is a dead tree. A man who has no traditional roots isn't very much alive. One of the most fascinating things about the modern city of Rome is the manner in which it has blended the old with the new. You can see beautiful tall modern apartments and office buildings and at the same time see a wall which dates back to before the time of Christ.

Because a tradition is old doesn't make it good nor does it make it bad. Just because Jesus rode on a donkey doesn't mean you are going to choose one as your means of transportation. You leave the donkeys to the past, but the ethical teachings of Jesus are just as current today as they were two thousand years ago. How can anyone improve on such teachings as: "Love thy God . . . and thy neighbor, as thyself," and "Do unto others as ye would have them do unto you?"

Don't divorce yourself from the past or live in the past, but blend the best of the old with the best of the new. In this way you will be able to live amiably with your parents, and also be a "sharp" dad or mom to your teenage child.

How can you meet some of the problems which your historic past has created for you? This is a very serious question to many. They are suffering for something over which they had no control. Perhaps you have inherited a bad family name or some other misfortune has been your lot. Always remember this: You may suffer from the sins of your fathers, but you are not responsible for the sins of your fathers. Don't allow anyone to place the guilt upon you. You are accountable to society for your own actions, but not for the deeds of your father, grandfather, great-grandfather, or any other relative.

THE PROBLEM OF FAMILY NAME
AND REPUTATION

The problem of family name and reputation is especially relevant to those who live in small towns and rural communities. The best thing you can do if you live in a community that never forgets is to leave.

One of the finest people I know is a young man who was born

out of wedlock. His mother lived in a small town where he was born and raised. When he was two years of age his mother married and later had two other children. The people in this narrow-minded community would never forget the fact the boy was an illegitimate child. It was thrown in his face so much that when he graduated from high school he left the town.

One day he came to see me about learning self-hypnosis. During the course of our conversation he related the emotional trials he had experienced. He also expressed some of the doubts and misgivings he had in his mind as a result of this cruel treatment. "I wish I knew who my real dad is. Am I basically bad because I don't have a father? Why do some people still call my mother a whore? Why can't people forget?" These are just a few of the questions asked by this young man. I told him there isn't any such thing as an illegitimate child. There might be illegitimate parents, but a baby certainly couldn't be illegitimate. He had as much right to life as anyone else. I also told him to forget about trying to learn who his real father was. His real father is the father who loved him and provided for him since he was two. As to his mother, I told him to love and respect her no matter what anyone said. He knew his mother was good, and this was the important thing.

Don't worry about your family background. Everyone has got a horse thief or some other type of rascal in his family lineage. The important thing is not who and what your ancestors were, but who and what you are. Jesus had two prostitutes, at least one adulteress, a murderer, and a few other unsavory characters in his family line. In fact, he himself was considered illegitimate by his contemporaries. Yet he became the greatest man the world has ever known.

LIVING WITH YOUR PAST PERSONAL LIFE

Let us now consider how you can effectively live with your personal past life. All of you have made mistakes, achieved victories, been hurt, and suffered traumas in your lifetime. The manner in which you relate yourself to the past determines what your future will be. If you harbor a bitter, resentful attitude about what has transpired in your life, this attitude will project itself into your future. That is, unless you do something about it, and change it. If the past has made you strong in character and positive in faith, then this will also project into your future. It is most important you learn how to live with your past. Your past, like everything else, can be divided into two general categories: the good things and the bad things of the past.

Three steps to follow regarding the past: There are three steps you should follow in dealing with the distasteful events of your past life. (1) You should leave them in the past. (2) You should learn to live with them. (3) You should laugh at the humor which is resident in every adverse circumstance. As you examine these three steps in detail, as follows, you will find them to be sufficient to enable you to live with the distresses of your yesteryears.

As much as possible, leave your bad experiences where they belong, in the past. That which is written is written, you can't change it. Leave the skeletons where they belong—in the closet. Don't try to undo the past. You can't! It is impossible!

It is not uncommon to come into contact with people who are extremely bitter about the past. They are bitter about mates who have divorced them, loved ones who have died, money and positions they have lost, or physical injuries they have suffered. All of these grievances could be summarized in the word, 'lost'— lost mates, lost loved ones, lost money, lost positions,-lost abilities, lost physical capabilities.

If you happen to fall into this bitter classification, you are bitter because you lost something or someone. You have lost something you can't get back, and the more you try to get it back the more bitter you become. The logical way to approach this problem is to stop trying to retrieve what you have lost, but replace it with something as similar to the original as possible. If you feel that what you lost can't be replaced, just accept the loss and learn to live with it.

In my ministry I have witnessed some heartbreaking events. I have seen the cold hand of death touch little babies, teenagers, parents in the prime of life, and the elderly. It has been my task to try and comfort men who have lost everything financially. Rebuilding the crushed egos of the divorced has also been allotted to me. These, plus many other calamities, are a part of every clergyman's ministry. Some individuals accept the misfortunes of life and make a wonderful adjustment. Others become extremely bitter. The pity is, they hurt themselves more than anyone else. Their bitterness also affects everyone else who is close to them. In a very real sense, their life comes to a halt because, in order to stay bitter, they have to constantly dwell on the past event which has distressed them so greatly. They literally live in the past, and therefore their hope of the future is very dim.

Some years ago I had as a client a woman whose whole life was devoted to hating her former husband. This was all she wanted to discuss. To her, he was a ratfink, a plain rat, a no-good rat and many other lovely names I will omit. As far as she was concerned, he was the most despicable creature on the face of God's Earth. She was telling me all this, even though she had been divorced for over ten years. During these ten years, she had made life miserable for herself, for him, for their children, and for everyone involved.

I asked her what she had accomplished with her life since the divorce. She told me she was getting even. "Getting even," I said, "everytime you hurt him, you are hurting yourself twice as much. You haven't got him back, and you won't. You are so bitter you can't keep friends. You can't keep a job. And above all, you haven't even started to build a new life for yourself. All you have accomplished in the last ten years is nothing. You have wasted ten years of your life in an effort of futility. No one ever gets even. You might hurt someone, but you hurt yourself more."

She proceeded to tell me she didn't want the old so-and-so back, and she was going to continue to harm him in every way she could. Her purpose in coming to me was to get rid of depression, which she felt had nothing to do with her former husband. Well, to make a long story short, I told her it would be a waste of her money and my time to see her any more. I dislike doing this to anyone, but when someone is so bent on ruining their own life and the life of someone else there is little you can do to help them.

Self-hypnosis can help you forget the past. It can at least take away the emotional hurt of past events. Hypnotize yourself and tell yourself: "I will think less and less about this event. I wish to be happy and at peace with myself; therefore, soon I will think of only good things from my past."

Leaving distressing events in the past is difficult when you harbor bitterness in your soul. It is also difficult if you "beat yourself" because of something you have done in the past. Guilt and remorse serve a positive purpose at times, but this is only true when there is a genuine reason for you to feel guilty. Once the guilt is experienced and acknowledged by a repentant attitude there is no longer any need for guilt.

It is possible that you have hurt someone and because of this you feel a strong need to punish yourself. Often this is more on a subconscious than on a conscious level. Perhaps ten, twenty, thirty or more years have gone by since the event took place, but you still continue to beat and punish yourself. This, of course, doesn't in any way help rectify whatever wrong you did.

A guilt complex relieved by self-hypnosis: A striking example of self-punishment is a client of mine who was punishing herself because she felt guilty about circumstances surrounding her father's death. The lady was in her late sixties, and her father had been dead for twenty-eight years, yet the guilt she felt was causing her a tremendous amount of distress. She was literally beating herself physically, emotionally, spiritually, and in every other conceivable way. When I asked her why she felt partially responsible for her father's death, she replied that there wasn't any one specific reason.

He had been sick for a number of years, and she had cared for him during his illness. Even though she tried to avoid it, resentment kept creeping into her heart. She resented having to wait on him. She resented the money which was being spent on his medical care. There were other children in the family, but they all refused to give very much assistance. My client was the youngest child and the favorite of the father, and therefore he chose to live with her and her family.

On the morning of the day the father died there was no indication that he was worse; in fact, he seemed to be the same as he had been for a number of months. It was on this morning that she felt she had had it. She had to get out of the house. It didn't make any difference to her what she did, as long as she could get away for a few hours. She made arrangements to have her neighbor watch her father while she went downtown to have lunch and do a little window shopping. During the time she was gone, her father died suddenly.

It was a combination of all these factors that created the guilt which had devastated her all these years. I told her that I didn't feel her guilt was necessary. She hadn't done anything to contribute to her father's death, but had really done more than her share in caring for him. The fact that she was away when he died was irrelevant. He would have died anyway. There was nothing she could have done to prevent it. Her resentment was natural. We all entertain thoughts of resentment at one time or another. The important thing is that we acknowledge the resentment and rid ourselves of it. All these years of self-punishment were completely unnecessary. Her own life and the lives of her loved ones were hurt and hindered by her warped attitudes and ideas.

I endeavored to strengthen this lady's faith in the five different ways we have mentioned, and I gave her positive hypnotic suggestions concerning this specific situation. After a few weeks, she had made a wonderful adjustment to life. She said, "I feel as if a great burden has been lifted from me and life once again has real meaning."

There is one other thing I want to mention in regard to leaving bad things in the past. Don't always blame the past for the wrongs you are doing today. I know, and I think all intelligent people accept the fact that our early years, our parents, our social environment all play a part in molding our personalities and our characters. Sometimes these early experiences create an abnormal behavior pattern which can cause an individual a tremendous amount of distress and sorrow. I bear this fact in mind when I say, don't always blame the past for your present difficulties. No matter what your personal past has been, you are morally responsible for your present behavior.

It is all too common for someone to commit a terrible crime and say, "I did it because my mother dropped me on my head when I was three months old." This example might seem a little ridiculous, but it nonetheless illustrates the point. All of us could find something in our pasts that we could cry about if we wanted. We could all feel sorry for ourselves. But this sort of attitude will only harm us; it won't help us.

As much as possible leave your bad experiences in the past. Don't be bitter about them. Don't beat yourself over something that happened years ago. And don't always blame the past for your present misfortunes.

Benefits from bad experiences: One of the great benefits of your bad experiences are the lessons you learn from them. Perhaps I should say, the lessons you should learn from them, because you don't always seem to learn from the past. When you don't learn, it is because you aren't perceptive enough. You aren't paying attention. There is an old adage which says: "When a dog bites you the first time it isn't your fault. If the dog bites you again, it is your fault." Don't make the same mistake twice. Learn your lesson well the first time you attend the school of hard knocks. To repeat the same course in this school could be disastrous.

Another reason why you sometimes don't learn from the past is that you receive pleasure from being hurt. If you didn't receive some kind of gratification from it, you wouldn't do it. The little boy who falls in the same muddy ditch every day does so because he likes to get muddy. He also likes the attention he gets from his mother. Women who never get their housework done and never have dinner ready on time are like this little boy. So is the man who hits the bars on the way home, and always forgets his wife's birthday. If this happens to be your plight, learn to get your pleasure in a more positive and constructive manner. Begin to learn from the past. An old proverb says, "we are too late smart, and too soon old."

You can learn from your past failures and hurts. Learn what not to do, and learn what to do. Examine your experiences to see if there is a discernible failure pattern in them. Do you repeat the same mistake or mistakes? If you discover that you do, take immediate action to initiate change in your life. This one simple thing can reverse the downward trend of your life.

Most men who fail repeatedly in business usually make the same mistakes every time. A client of mine had been in business six different times and had flunked out six times. He always made the same error: The business would be doing well, and he would get delusions of grandeur. He would overexpand, bite off more than he could chew, and lose the business. There were some valuable lessons from these experiences which he wasn't learning. One, he was a capable small businessman, but he didn't know how to cope effectively with the personnel problems of a large operation. Second, he enjoyed pioneering new businesses, but he became bored when the business was established. He needed challenge, but he sometimes took on more challenge than he could handle. Third, he failed repeatedly because of the attention he received. People noticed him. They felt sorry for him. His wife would pamper and pet him until he was over his hurt.

This same truth also applies to people who are always getting hurt. I guess we could say they have a "hurt pattern," for they always manage to get themselves in situations where they will be hurt. A case in point is that of a lady who had been divorced three times, and was about to do it again. She told me about her marriages, her husbands, and how they had all betrayed her. After seeing her for a number of weeks, I pointed out to her she had married the same personality type in each of her marriages. All of her husbands were the flashy, unstable, playboy type. She knew this when she married them. Why did she do this? Why did she repeat the same "hurt pattern" over and over again? Well, she liked the excitement. She liked the romance of it all. She liked the arguments. She enjoyed the sympathy her friends gave her during and after the divorce. Basically, she was immature and didn't know how to build a lasting relationship with a mature man.

Learn to laugh at bad experiences: You should not only leave bad experiences in the past and learn valuable lessons from them, but you should also learn to laugh at them. If you look for it, you can find something humorous in even the most trying situations. When you are able to laugh at the bad things of the past, you have reached the plateau of victory. The negative emotions of the past—fear, worry, and anxiety—no longer enslave you. Laugh at the devil, and he will flee from thee! It is always better to laugh than it is to cry.

A client of mine was having a difficult time adjusting to a reconciliation with her husband. Her husband had been involved with another woman for about three years. She had been aware of the affair for a number of months before it ended. During those months there had been endless quarrels and fights. Finally, they had decided to end it. But after they had gone to the expense of paying legal and court fees, they agreed to try it all over again.

They remarried and everything went quite well except for the fact that she couldn't forget her husband's escapades. I told her I knew this must be difficult for her, but the marriage would be in danger if she couldn't desensitize herself in regard to those happenings. I asked her if she ever stopped to think of how ridiculous her husband must have looked while he was sneaking around like a teenage boy. He had really made a fool of himself. She mentioned one occasion when she caught him in a big lie. For a moment she was silent, then she started laughing. "That was the poorest lie I ever heard," she said. This was just a start. Hypnosis was used on her for a number of weeks until she was able to live with the past.

Building on past good experiences: We have discussed the bad things of the past, but what about the good things? You, no doubt, have had successful, memorable, happy days in the past. Well, don't lean on them, but build on them. A man who lives in the past, be it good or bad, will never relate himself very well to the present or the future. You can be sure that the individual who is always talking about what he has done isn't doing anything now.

Use your triumphant moments of the past to inspire you. When King David of Israel was a shepherd boy, he was called upon to fight a giant named Goliath. He inspired himself by saying, "I have slain a lion and a bear, and God will deliver the Philistine into my hands." Mother, you have raised your children; therefore you can be successful in the business world if you wish. Father, you have built a business or you have been successful in your position; therefore, you can meet the new challenge in your life.

Also use the good of the past to instruct you. You can learn from bad experiences, but you learn more from the good ones. Successful experience is your best teacher. Sit long in this school and learn your lessons well. Never slight your friend, good experience. Never give him up for some inferior newcomer. Good experience will introduce you to many new friends, but always meet them through him.

Use the memory of your good times of the past to sustain you during the difficult times of the present. A friend of mine, who was a prisoner of war during the Second World War, said that he kept his hopes alive by thinking of pleasant scenes from his past. At times life seemed unbearable, but during these torment-ing moments he recalled experiences from his boyhood at home. He said he especially remembered visits to his grandfather's farm. The memory of the fresh air, the open fields, the good food, and the sage advice of his grandparents made it possible for him to endure the rigors of the prison life.

You can live with your past and you can have faith in the past if you will apply the principles of faith given in Chapter 10. Look to the past in a positive, realistic manner. Limit your faith according to the object of faith. Then project your faith into the future. Tomorrow is yours!

SELF-HYPNOSIS SUGGESTION
FOR LIVING WITH THE PAST

Because I want a (insert your own P.D.E.M.) I will leave bad experiences in the past. I will also learn valuable lessons from them and be able to laugh at them. I will build on my good experiences.

HIGHLIGHTS TO REMEMBER FROM THIS CHAPTER:

1. You have two pasts: a historic past and a personal past.
2. There are three attitudes you can have toward your historic past.
   (1) You can deny it and try to forget it.
   (2) You can live in the past.
   (3) You can blend the good of the old with the good of the new.
3. You may suffer from the sins of your fathers, but you are not responsible for them.
4. Your attitude toward the past will determine your attitude toward the future.
5. There are three things you should do when dealing with the bad experiences of the past.
   (1) Leave them in the past. Don't be bitter. Don't beat your-self. Don't blame the past.
   (2) Learn from them.
   (3) Laugh at them.

6. There are five things you should do with the good experiences of your past.
   (1) Build upon them.
   (2) Use them to inspire you.
   (3) Use them to instruct you.
   (4) Use them to sustain you.
   (5) Use the principles of faith found in Chapter 10 to increase your confidence in the past.
7. A self-hypnosis suggestion is given for living with the past.

14

HOW SELF-HYPNOSIS
CAN ENHANCE
YOUR MARRIAGE

MOST PEOPLE ARE ASTOUNDED BY the fact that about one out of four marriages eventually ends up in divorce. The thing which amazes me, however, is that more of them don't end there. The greater portion of married people *are enduring their marriages; they aren't enjoying them.* Self-hypnosis can be of immense value in adding pleasure and peace to your marriage.

THE PSYCHOLOGICAL DIFFERENCES IN THE SEXES

Let me explain why I am amazed that the divorce rate in our country isn't any higher than it is. The first reason is the basic anthropological, cultural, emotional, and perceptive differences which exist between the male and female. Very few men ever understand the female of the species. We laugh and joke about it but it isn't a joke; it is a fact. The other side of this picture is seldom discussed, but is just as prevalent. Very few women understand the male of the species. The differences in the sexes are more psychological than they are physical.

The physical distinctions were made by God, but the psychological differences have been molded by man. It is the psychological factor which causes disharmony in the marriage. The man who never shows concern, patience, thoughtfulness, or kindness toward his wife isn't going to have a wife very long. The woman who doesn't make her husband feel like the modern counterpart of the ancient cave man isn't going to have him around very long. True, he isn't out fighting dinosaurs, but he is out earning the bread. The woman isn't the weaker sex, but in most situations she wants to be treated as such. And if you are a smart husband you will show her the consideration she desires. You will open the car door, the house door, etc. for her. You will seat her, especially in public places. Maybe you have been married for twenty years and haven't done this in the last nineteen years. Do it and see what happens! If she doesn't drop dead, she will mature into the sweetest wife possible. Your husband might not be Hercules in bed, but if you want to keep him, you'd better act as if he is. Your wife might not be the most beautiful woman in the world, but you had better act as if she is.

SOCIOLOGICAL DIFFERENCES DIMINISHING

The sociological differences between the sexes are diminishing with each generation. A few hundred years ago, a married woman wouldn't venture out of her house unescorted. She could not make an appearance or say a word without permission when her husband was entertaining guests in their home. Women have gained more rights in the last sixty years than in all the previous years of history. These new liberties have created a new feminine image. A woman can now come and go as she pleases. She has the same educational opportunities as the male. The right to vote is hers. If she doesn't want to live with a man, she can divorce him. She can work, and in many instances is paid wages comparable to earnings of the male. The perfection of birth-control methods, the upgrading of jobs and pay for the woman, and continued educational opportunities in the near future will further decrease the sociological and psychological differences between the sexes.

THE LACK OF PREPARATION FOR MOST MARRIAGES

The second reason why I am amazed the divorce rate doesn't go higher is because of the lack of preparation for marriage.

Would the Army send your son to war without first teaching him how to shoot a rifle? Would you allow your daughter to fly an airplane without first giving her instructions? The answer to both of the questions is, NO. You would do nothing which would bring harm to your child. But stop and think for a moment. You educate your child for business, but do you educate your child for the most important thing in life? The marriage contract is the most binding contract they will ever sign. Yet how much do they know about the business of marriage? These terms might sound cold, but marriage is a legally binding contract. If you don't believe me, try to break it. The crying shame of the nation is the lack of proper educational courses in marriage and family living.

Let us now notice why some marriages fail, and what you can do to improve your marriage. Most divorces are the result of ignorance, immaturity, indifference, indiscretion, or interference.

If I were to place the major reason for the breakdown of marriages at the top of a list, it would be ignorance. The more I deal with human problems of all types, the more I am convinced of this fact. Ignorance is the number one enemy of marriage. As we have just noticed, the average person enters into matrimony without the slightest conception of what it is all about. He has no idea whatsoever about the responsibilities and trials of marriage. Many young people come to the marriage altar believing that overnight some magical power will take over in their lives. Because they are one, they will own all the big houses and cars they see married people possess in the movies.

Not too long ago I was counseling with a young couple for whom I was to perform the wedding rites. In the course of the conversation, I asked them where they were going to live. At first they planned to move into an apartment, but in a couple of years they intended to move to a rather exclusive part of town. The young man had a job which paid only a moderate wage, so I asked them how they were going to manage this. They didn't know. The young man said he didn't really care if he ever lived there. At this the bride-to-be let him know she *had* to live in that particular neighborhood. Right here were the seeds of a divorce. These two young people had no conception of the value of the dollar.

IGNORANCE OF FAMILY MONEY MANAGEMENT

Ignorance of family money management is a deadly enemy of good marriages. I believe that money problems are one of the major causes of divorce in the early years of marriage. It is often the root problem from which many other problems grow. This is especially true in situations when the family income is moderate and a number of children are born within a short span of time. The same thing happens to couples who have plenty of money and no children, but who have no sound family financial policy. They acquire more bills than they can meet. Then they begin to blame one another for the dilemma. You can buy a lot of things for a dollar down, but don't forget that the rest of the bill has to be paid. The thing that can sink your family budget is the accumulation of too many five, ten, and fifteen dollar payments per month. The American way of credit is a wonderful thing if you use common sense and don't abuse it.

I would hesitate to number the people I have interviewed whose debts, not including groceries, exceeded their income. Color televisions, power lawn mowers, stereos, hair dryers, tape recorders, and personal loans from finance companies head the average list of debts. Most of these items would not fall into the category of essentials. But these are the "little foxes" which can ruin you financially.

My advice to young couples would be: don't become house poor, car poor or appliance poor. Leave enough room in your budget to buy a hamburger once in awhile. Allow money for a vacation. These are the things which relieve some of your tensions and make life worth living.

Ignorance in family money management is just one kind of ignorance which can sink the ship of matrimony. There are many other deadly torpedoes which can do their destructive work just as well. Ignorance in sexual matters, ignorance of child behavior, and ignorance in the basics of human relationship are just a few of the many areas which could be mentioned. All of these things could be overcome with the right kind of education. And this education must begin in the home. Be honest with your children. Be optimistic as well as realistic with them. Give them responsibility equivalent to their age. Don't unload all the facts of life on them when they are five years old, but answer their questions in an intelligent manner when they ask them. Give them a good emotional and spiritual foundation on which they can build their lives and marriages.

IMMATURITY IN MARRIAGE

Another cause of divorce is immaturity. There are some people who just never seem to grow up. They might be thirty, forty, fifty, or sixty years old physically, but emotionally they are about eight, ten, or twelve. When their mate won't play the game their way or dance to their tune, they are ready to call it quits. With them it is a matter of always being on the receiving end, but never on the giving end. The female of this type usually goes home to mother, the male quite often finds his solace in the bottle. It is really a shame people get married before they mature, because it creates nothing but grief and sorrow for themselves and all concerned.

I once counseled with a young husband who couldn't or wouldn't make a decision without first asking his father what he should do. There is, of course, nothing wrong with this practice if it is kept in bounds. But this fellow wouldn't make *any* decisions without dad. And what father said was final. Furthermore, he never asked his wife for her opinion, and if she offered it, she was told to keep her mouth shut. Well she shut her mouth, but she opened a divorce action!

Another example of immaturity is that of a young wife and mother who just couldn't adapt herself to any responsibilities or work. The husband would put in a hard day's work and then come home, cook dinner, clean house, and do the wash. The only thing the young mother could do was to take care of the baby "properly." The marriage went along smoothly as long as the husband did her work, but when he became tired of this routine she was ready to put the brute out into the street.

These people are extremely neurotic and make very poor marriage partners. As long as you feed their neurosis and play their game, the marriage will continue, but God help you when you rock the boat and stop fulfilling their every wish.

Outside interference plays a strong part in the destruction of many marriages. It is difficult for parents to sit back and allow their newly wed son or daughter to make their mistakes. But believe me, you had better sit back. If you are asked for advice and counsel give it. But if you are not asked, keep it to yourself. Allow your children to build and live their own lives. If you want to be appreciated, keep your distance. The marriage you save might be the marriage of your child.

Once you are married you are no longer obligated to obey your parents. You should honor and respect them, but you don't have to obey them. Your first allegiance is to your mate.

A couple in their early fifties came to me for counseling because of interference on the part of the husband's mother. This couple had been married for ten years, and no children were involved. The man showed preference for his mother over his wife in everything. The wife had hoped, prayed and worked for a good marriage, but it never transpired. There was no willingness for change on the part of the husband. He thought his wife was jealous and unreasonable. He said he loved his wife, but he also loved his mother. He might have loved both women, but his love for both was abnormal.

How shall your marriage survive if you are indifferent to your mate? Believe me, it won't! You might have a marriage in name and appearance, but that is all you will have. Indifference is the deadly enemy of marriages which have lasted for a period of ten years or more. Don't take your mate for granted, lest someone else take him for real! Plants, animals, or anything else which are neglected, die. The same thing is true of marriage—if you don't work at it and cultivate it, it will die.

The husband who is never home, and when he is home falls asleep in his favorite easy chair, always seem shocked when his wife confronts him with a divorce. "What have I done! Haven't I been a good husband! Haven't I earned a living and paid the bills . . ." It isn't so much what he has done which is causing his marital trouble, as what he hasn't done. He hasn't paid attention to his wife. Usually he has neglected her sexually and socially. Home is a place where he occasionally eats and sleeps.

To him, his wife has no particular identity. She is a cook, housekeeper, or governess, but not a person. Because she has suppressed her feelings, he thinks she has no feelings. He honors her once in awhile with a quick peck on the cheek. When he does desire sex he expects his wife to be the "instant lover."

The other side of the picture is the wife who is so engrossed in her children, her clubs, or her charities she doesn't have time for hubby. He is a great guy who watches the kids and pays the bills. He doesn't really care about sex or even being alone with her too often.

Then the fatal moment comes when he meets someone who pays attention to him, and makes him feel like he is a person. The wife just can't figure out where she missed the mark. She did her best. Yes, she did her best in everything except her marriage.

Neglect your marriage, and you will destroy it!

Indiscretion is another factor which often leads to the downfall of marriage. The mate who gets a big bang out of embarrassing his mate in public will someday get his. Usually the thing he gets is a divorce or a frigid wife. A husband or wife can often be reconciled to many bad situations, but they seldom can stand the humiliation of public embarrassment. Even the wounds of an affair can be healed, provided the offender isn't too indiscreet. But the more people who know about the affair, the harder it is to live with.

USING HYPNOSIS TO AVOID THE FIVE DANGEROUS "I'S"

Avoid these five dangerous "I's": ignorance, immaturity, interference, indifference and indiscretion if you wish to maintain a happy marriage. Use self-hypnosis to improve yourself in any of the areas where you see it necessary. Here are seven things you can do to improve your marriage.

1. *Be sure you fully understand what marriage is and what it involves.* Marriage is two things: It is a contract, and it is a communication. I have already mentioned that the marriage contract is the most binding, demanding contract you will ever sign. It is a contract which involves yourself, your mate, your God, the state, your children, and sometimes your religious establishment. Do not take this contract lightly. If you do, you won't be married very long. If you honor the contract in good faith your marriage will last.

Marriage is also a communication. This is a fact that is stressed very strongly by psychologists and marriage counselors. Now let me show you how psychology and religion blend beautifully in this matter. Theologians sometimes refer to marriage as a communion. The words communication and communion have a common derivation. They both come from the Latin word, "communis." Basically both words mean to have in common or to share. Where there is no communion in marriage there will be no communication. Verbal conversation, alone, is not communication! Communication in marriage goes far beyond mere talking—it is a spiritual, social, and sexual communion of the personalities of two people. These three factors are interrelated. One factor depends on the other factors. A good marriage is a marriage where there is communion and communication.

2. *Be sure you fully understand the nature of love.* Very few people do! What do you mean when you say, "I love him or I love her?" The word "love" is difficult to define, but there are three Greek words which can be rendered as love in our language which will help you to understand its meaning. They are: eros, phileo, and agapa. Eros refers to the sensual, sexual expression of love. In fact, Eros was the name of one of the Grecian gods of love. The Romans later borrowed this god and called him Cupid. I imagine you have heard of Cupid and his arrows. Perhaps you have even been shot by him a few times. Most marriages, to begin with, are based on eros. The first attraction you have toward your mate is a physical, sexual attraction.

Sex is a vital part of marriage, but a marriage which is formed solely on the basis of sex will not last. The laws of nature are against it. Too much emphasis is placed upon sex in marriage. A normal marriage must have it, but it is only one aspect of the communication of marriage.

I have counseled with numerous women whose husbands have beaten them half to death. They took this and continued to live with them. But when the husband went to bed with another woman, this was the end. Like all men, I don't completely understand the female's thinking processes, but if I were a woman the reason for divorce would be reversed.

The word, phileo, means deep affection. This describes the love you might have for a close friend or a relative.

The word agapa means divine love. This is the word used in

John 3:16 to describe God's love for humanity. It means that God loved us despite the facts that we were unlovable, that we didn't desire his love, and that we couldn't reciprocate his love. The expression of this love is in God's giving. When we apply this to marital love it means we stay married not only "because of" but also "despite." You love your husband not only because he is nice, kind, etc., but also despite the fact that he is late for dinner, and despite the fact that he forgets your birthday. You love your wife not only because she is sweet and desirable, but you also love her despite the fact that she spends too much money and nags you once in awhile. The expression of your agapa is in giving. If you give one hundred per cent of yourself to your marriage, you will usually receive a one hundred per cent return from it.

I believe these three Greek words describe the evolution of a good marriage. It begins with eros. It buds into phileo. And it blossoms into agapa.

3. *Be sure your mate feels loved by you.* This is the most important aspect of your marriage. Your spouse can overlook and overcome many things if he feels you love him. You can give your husband or wife the assurance of your love in two ways.

The first way is by declaring your love verbally. When was the last time you told your mate that you love her? You might say, "I don't have to tell her I love her. She knows I love her." You might think she knows it, but I'll guarantee she would like you to tell her you love her once in awhile. The same thing is true of the husband. He likes to be told by his wife that he is loved. People in every phase of life need reassurance. The three little words, "I love you," can work miracles in your marriage.

The second way to make your spouse feel loved is to demonstrate your love. Show him you love him by deeds of kindness and consideration. Remember important dates, especially your anniversary. There are so many ways that you can express your love, but one of the most important things is the little common courtesies of daily life. Declare your love and demonstrate your love, and you will develop a strong and happy marriage.

4. *Stay young in your mind and body.* It is appalling the way some married people allow their physical appearance to "go to

pot." Many wives don't take the time to maintain a neat attractive appearance. Their hair is dirty and uncurled, and their figures are saggy and sloppy. It only takes a few minutes per day to be clean and well-groomed. In fact, it is easier to be clean than to be dirty. You will keep your husband the same way you got him. One of the most important factors in getting him was your appearance. A few minutes a day spent in doing a few basic exercises can keep your figure in good shape until the day of your death. Your food intake also plays a vital part in maintaining your figure. Eat a moderate, well balanced diet, and you will have no problems. This advice applies to the husband as well as to the wife. For your health's sake as well as your marriage's sake, get rid of your excess weight. Watch the calories and get a moderate amount of exercise.

Also stay young in mind. With the exception of senility, age is an attitude of mind. By staying young in mind, I don't mean you should try to think like a teenager or a college kid. I mean that you should keep your mind vital and alive. Be informed concerning the tremendous issues which confront our generation. Read a good variety of books, magazines, and newspapers. Develop the mind power God has given you.

Did you ever stop to think how erudite you would be if you read fifty pages a day? This should take thirty to sixty minutes of your time. You would average reading one book per week or fifty-two books per year. In ten years, you would read five hundred and twenty books. If you do this you will be as informed as the average college professor, provided you read the right books.

5. Add new dimensions and experiences to your marriage. Don't settle for a humdrum existence. Plan to take a second honeymoon about twice a year. It doesn't have to take a lot of money, and if you watch your budget you can make provisions for a couple of week-end trips.

Enlarge your circle of friends. Make an effort to acquire friends outside of your present group. This will prove to be stimulating intellectually as well as socially.

Don't go to the same place on every vacation. Some people go to the same place every year. Explore a little. Travel together and visit new places and learn how others live.

6. *Be realistic about your mate.* Remember, don't place un-limited faith in him or her. Don't look for perfection. Everyone has his faults; therefore make allowances for them in your hus-band or wife. If you have a realistic faith in your mate, you won't fall apart when you learn he isn't a knight in shining armor or she isn't a fairy princess.

7. *Build a life together but don't lose your personal identity.* Too much togetherness can be as harmful as not enough to-getherness. The husband or wife who builds an entire life around the mate is extremely foolish. What if your marriage does end in divorce? If your whole life is built upon your mate, you will be lost. It is, therefore, important that you maintain your per-sonal identity and have interests of your own. This is important to you and to your marriage. You can suffocate a marriage with too much togetherness. No man wants to take his wife with him all the time, and no wife wants her husband with her every moment.

Here are six things you should do together:

(1) Grow together
(2) Play together
(3) Love together
(4) Work together
(5) Worship together
(6) Talk together

Marriage is a vital living union of two people joined in a mutual communion. You must work and pray to keep it vibrant and meaningful.

SELF-HYPNOSIS SUGGESTION TO HELP YOU ENHANCE YOUR MARRIAGE

Because (insert your own P.D.E.M.) I will give my best to maintain a vital vibrant marriage. I am understanding, kind, and considerate of my mate at all times. Each day my love for my mate grows stronger.

HIGHLIGHTS TO REMEMBER FROM THIS CHAPTER:

1. Two reasons why I am amazed the divorce rate is not higher than it is:

(1) The basic anthropological, cultural, emotional, and perceptive differences between the sexes.

(2) The lack of preparation for marriage.

2. Five major factors which cause divorce:

(1) Ignorance

(2) Immaturity

(3) Interference

(4) Indifference

(5) Indiscretion

3. Seven things you can do to maintain and enhance your marriage.

(1) Be sure you fully understand the nature of marriage. Marriage is a contract and a communication.

(2) Be sure you fully understand the nature of love.

(3) Be sure your mate feels loved by you.

(4) Stay young in mind and body.

(5) Add need dimensions and experiences to your marriage.

(6) Be realistic about your mate.

(7) Build a life together but don't lose your personal identity.

4. A self-hypnosis suggestion is given for enhancing your marriage.

15

HOW SELF-HYPNOSIS CAN HELP YOU TO BE FINANCIALLY SUCCESSFUL

SUCCESS, WHAT IS IT? SUCCESS, who is one? Success, how do you become one? Where do you buy it? Does it come in a bottle? Can you learn it in a success course? Most success courses are taught by men who aren't too successful. Can you become a success by reading a book? More books are written about this subject than any other on the market today. Everyone wants to be successful. Everyone wants to be a success. Those who are successful want to be more successful. The greatest sin of our age is not to be successful. You wife won't love you, and your children won't respect you, or at least that's the way the books read.

THE TRUE MEANING OF SUCCESS

Now let us try to answer some of these questions. It is possible to be successful without being a success. And it is possible to be a success without being successful. A man could successfully commit a crime: bank robbery, murder, rape, etc. and not be a success. He is a successful criminal, but I, at least, wouldn't consider him a success. It is possible for a man not to be outstandingly successful in any one thing and still be a success in his life. Perhaps he has only an ordinary run of the mill job and is worth only a moderate sum of money. But his life has depth and meaning. He is endeavoring to better himself, but in the meantime he has self-confidence and is at peace with himself. His relationship with his wife and children is warm and genuine. Friends praise him, and his enemies find it difficult to hate him. This man is a success, and it is just a matter of time until he will be financially successful.

I know people, and I am sure you are acquainted with many, who are successful in one or two phases of their lives. But these same people are miserable failures in the more important aspects of life. Some of your most successful business men are abject failures in their personal lives. As husbands and fathers, they get a great big fat rating of zero. They might know the stock market, but they don't know their own children. Oh, they know who they are, but they don't know their needs and desires.

A success is an individual who is living a meaningful and useful life. His life has consistency and balance. He is "successful" in most areas of his life in contrast to being successful in only one or two areas. He performs a task which he has chosen and which he enjoys. His income is adequate to meet all of his as well as his family's needs. His relationship with his fellowman is good, because he exercises a positive realistic faith in all of its five directions.

If you will put into practice the teachings of this book you will be a success in *your life*. It is my purpose in this chapter to give you some vital information as to how you can become more successful in your work. I want to teach you how you can acquire a larger income in order that you and your loved ones might enjoy all the good things of life. God wants you to have these things, and I want to help you obtain them through hypnosis.

The reason I have gone into quite a bit of detail in defining success is to point out the fact that you don't have to be a failure as a husband and father in order to be successful. There are people who blame their business failures on the fact that they couldn't neglect their families. This is indeed a poor excuse. Then there are people who blame their family failures on their business success. This, too, is a poor excuse. A man who is a success finds time and talent to do everything in his life which needs to be done. And what he does, he does well.

HOW SELF-HYPNOSIS AIDS IN FINANCIAL SUCCESS

Self-hypnosis can be a tremendous aid in bringing you financial success. A number of people who have taken my self-hypnosis course have bettered themselves financially. In an average class of fifteen or twenty, there will always be two or three who will testify concerning an increase in income or an advancement in position. I have had some people who have gone into business for themselves as a result of the course. When they first told me of their plans, it frightened me, but as yet all of them have been more than successful in their efforts. I firmly believe that when self-hypnosis is properly used, it can be an effective tool in increasing your income and advancing your business or career.

No one can make you an overnight success, but here are some constructive ideas which you can use to increase your capabilities.

1. Know where you are going: Remember, your subconscious is a goal-striving mechanism. Give it a reasonable goal, and it will achieve it. You must be thoroughly convinced of this fact, in order for it really to be effective in achieving your success. I was recently working with a young real-estate salesman during a slump period in his sales. He came to me purely out of curiosity. He didn't believe he could be hypnotized, and he thought the whole concept of hypnosis helping anyone to sell was a lot of "bunk."

Fortunately, he turned out to be a good hypnotic subject and went into deep hypnosis on his first visit. This convinced him of the possibilities of what might be done. On a subsequent visit, we proceeded to set monthly sales goals. The month prior to his seeing me he had sold nothing. I had him choose his own sales goal. He thought awhile, and finally decided that he should consummate six "deals" a month. The goal was a little high for this time of the year, but he needed to do this much business every month to meet all his financial obligations.

While under hypnosis, I had him visualize the amount of money this would mean to him every month. I suggested to him that his subconscious would work on his behalf to form this idea of the mind into a reality. He was also instructed to hypnotize himself each day and give himself this sales-goal. The following week he closed two "deals." In two and one half weeks he fulfilled his goal of six "deals" for the first month. Needless to say, this man is now sold on the idea of hypnosis in selling.

I have had numerous salesmen take my course as individuals, but as yet I haven't been able to sell the idea to any large sales organization, despite the fact that I guarantee that the course will pay for itself by increasing sales or it will cost the firm absolutely nothing. I mention this to point out how prejudice and fear hinder progress in regard to the use of hypnosis.

Whenever I teach something about goals to my classes, I invariably have one or two students who will say, "Everyone talks about goals. That's nothing new." This is true, almost every training course emphasizes goals, but *only* a self-hypnosis course can tell you how to reach your goals. When we talk about goals in relationship to hypnosis and the subconscious, we are standing on good, solid, scientific ground.

Give yourself the goal; feed it into your subconscious, and you will reach it. Know where you want to go in your career.

2. Give yourself a P.D.E.M. for the attaining of this particular goal. It is most important that you know why you want to make more money or have a better position. This is relatively easy to determine. Ask yourself, "What do I intend to do with the money? How will I feel when I get the new position?" If you want to put the money into a savings bank, your P.D.E.M. would be security. If you intend to set aside a major part of it for your children's education, then your P.D.E.M. would be the assured future of your children. Perhaps you want more money to see more of the world or retire at an early age. These things, in themselves, would constitute your P.D.E.M.

The reasons for desiring an advancement in position might be prestige, increased income, increased esteem in the eyes of your wife, etc. Anyone of these in themselves would be a very powerful P.D.E.M. When you are able to conceive a specific goal and ascertain exactly what is your P.D.E.M., you will be successful, provided you have programed your subconscious in the right manner. The rest of the ideas in this chapter will help you give yourself the proper programing.

3. Give yourself adequate preparation. Prepare yourself with the necessary educational qualifications and the proper mental attitude. Most of the men at the top are men who never cease to give themselves thorough preparation for every task which comes their way. A great man I once knew said ninety per cent of genius is hard work.

Prepare yourself with as much practical experience as possible. If you want to be a minister some day, start teaching a Sunday School class today. If you desire to be an engineering salesman in the future, start selling magazines or something today. No matter what field you choose, you can find something which you can do right now which will give you valuable, practical experience.

4. In order to succeed you must have determination of purpose. The successful man is the one who knows what is required of him and is willing to pay the price. He is the man who hangs on when everyone else gives up. He gets up every time he is knocked down. Men who fail are men who have no patience and no determination.

5. You must have self-confidence. You must believe in yourself. One of the common clichés among salesmen is, "I can sell anything I believe in." This sounds good, but I believe a good salesman should be able to sell anything. Believing in your product is without a doubt a valuable sales asset. But something far more important is that you believe in yourself and your abilities. If you don't believe you can succeed, you won't succeed until you change your attitude.

6. Think big! Give yourself a large goal. Then plan smaller daily, weekly and monthly goals which will eventually get you to the big goal. Be realistic, but always set your goal a little higher than you think you can go. Believe me! It is just as easy, many times, to get to the top as it is to stay at the bottom. Develop a larger, better self-image. Get out of the nickel and dime class and move forward and ahead. Remember, little men think little. Big men think big.

7. *You must be capable of making decisions.* You won't always make the right decision, but you must make the right decision at the right time most of the time. Indecision is the one thing which will ruin you faster than anything else. The individual who doesn't know whether or not he should expand his business or take on a new line or hire a particular person will never succeed. It is better to make a wrong decision than to make no decision. If you can't make decisions, it won't be long until you will lose the respect of those with whom you work. Soon someone else will be making your decisions, and he will also be sitting in your chair at your desk in what used to be your office.

Self-hypnosis can be a valuable aid in making decisions! The method I use is to hypnotize myself, then give my subconscious all of the pertinent facts associated with my decision. I tell my subconscious to deliver a decision to me in the next few hours or minutes, depending on the time factor. I then forget about it, and before long a definite course of action is impressed upon my mind. As yet, I have never gone wrong following this procedure. There have been times when I didn't follow the advice of my subconscious because it seemed rather far-fetched to me, and invariably I have regretted not following the choice it delivered to me.

8. *Harness the power of your imagination.* Put it to work for you. We have already discussed the importance and power of the imagination, but this knowledge will be useless unless you put it to work. To give just one example of how to use your imagination to help you succeed, imagine you are without a job. Think of the various things you could do to make a living without working for someone else. If you allow your imagination a few minutes to work on the problem it will come up with numerous ideas. This could be dangerous because you might think of something which will motivate you to quit your present job and go to work yourself.

9. *You must be willing to work hard.* Hard work alone won't make you wealthy or successful. You must have ideas, goals, P.D.E.M.'s, etc., but these things will be of no value unless you put them to work. You can't succeed if you are afraid of work.

Very few really successful men work an eight hour day. A lazy man is out of the running before the race begins. If you enjoy your work and learn how to work at top efficiency in a relaxed manner, hard work won't harm you in the least. You can learn to work in this relaxed manner through self-hypnosis. I am not inferring that you should work twenty-four hours a day, seven days a week. You must take time to relax and enjoy life, but you must be willing to work long and hard if you want success.

10. A successful person takes care of his problems as they arise. If you do not solve your small problems, it won't be long until they grow into big problems. You must develop the ability to distinguish between the problem situation, which is self-healing, and the one which needs your most astute attention. This ability comes only from experience. The man who is afraid to face and handle difficult situations cannot possibly succeed. There isn't a business or occupation which doesn't have its problems and headaches.

Quite often young ministers are disillusioned when they enter the pastorate, because of the pettiness, personality conflicts and cheap politics which exist in every congregation. It is amusing to me when I hear a businessman express the thought that he might someday give up the rat race of the business world and enter into the quiet peaceful life of the ministry. Believe me, he would be like a lamb cast into a den of wolves.

Your ability to face your problems as they arise will, to a great extent, determine whether or not you will be successful. There is no substitute for a backbone. To put it even more bluntly, you have to have *guts, gumption,* and *go* if you are to be a success.

11. If you are to be successful, you must not be governed by circumstances, but you must govern the circumstances. You don't wait for things to happen, you make things happen. The individual who is continually waiting for the sun to shine, or the market to pick up is never going to succeed. There are four common excuses which people give for their lack of initiative in striking down the narrow road which leads to success and prosperity. These excuses are classics. You hear them every day, as follows:

1. "You have to have money to make money." This sounds good and reasonable, but it isn't true. It is true to those who believe it, but only because they believe it. The fact is that most men who have made good on their own did it with a very small sum of money. After they got on their way, great sums of money were made available to them, but initially they started with little or no money. True, money is definitely a valuable asset, but *it is not essential*. If you have the ideas, the goals, the determination, and the willingness to work, the money you need will come to you. Act as if you already have the backing of millions of dollars. Play the role of a millionaire and see what happens.

2. "You have to have a great deal of education." I would be the last person to minimize the value of education. This is especially true for younger people. My advice is get all the education you can possibly acquire. But if you are older without too much education, don't believe the lie that you have to have education to succeed. There are still many areas of endeavor where an individual without too much education can make it. Also, remember that education is an unending process. You can educate yourself. It takes discipline and work, but it can be done.

3. "You have to have connections if you are to get ahead, It's who you know, and not what you know." This is no doubt true in certain situations, but most of the time it doesn't apply. Very few businesses are going to keep someone on their payroll at an executive level who doesn't produce. There are very few firms that will deny a man employment and advancement if he has the ability to make money for their firm.

As far as connections are concerned, I have found that very few men with the ability to help are willing to help. Don't ask for connections; make your own connections. If you need help from a certain source, don't look around for someone to introduce you. Introduce yourself! If you have something to offer that source, you are as important to it as it is to you. Never be afraid to approach anyone. They were made by the same Creator who created you. They are made out of the same dust you are made of. After all, the worse they can do is say, "No," and if you didn't call on them the answer would also be no as far as you are concerned.

4. "You can't make it by yourself." Once again there is some

degree of truth in this excuse. Everyone has to have the help and assistance of others in any life situation. But this is not what I am talking about at this time. There are men who are afraid to venture out on their own. They always feel they have to have a partner. Many times partnerships, etc. work out fine, but they are not essential. You don't have to have someone else. You can make it on your own, provided you believe in yourself. If you feel you need others in order to succeed, this indicates a lack of confidence and maturity on your part. Learn to stand alone on your own two feet. This will be the greatest day of your life if you haven't as yet developed this kind of confidence.

Avoid these four deceitful and fatal errors. Govern circumstances. Make things happen. The salesman who is always waiting for a better opportunity or a better prospect is going to starve unless he is on a salary. The executive who waits for opportunity to knock might have to wait a long time. Get to work and create your own opportunities. If you do this, and there is no room at the top, don't worry! They will make room for you!

12. Don't be afraid to make mistakes. Don't plan to make mistakes, but at the same time don't be afraid to make one. The man who never makes a mistake is the man who never does anything. To err is human. When you make a mistake, learn from it. Don't make the same one twice. Scientists make thousands of mistakes before they succeed. Failure is not defeat unless you accept it as such. Failure does not have to stop you unless you let it. It is an old proverb, but nonetheless true: you can lose a battle without losing the war.

13. You must be able to motivate others. A successful man is one who has the ability to get others to do their best for him. It's one thing to have people working for you; it is quite another thing to have them doing their best for you. Develop the talent of being able to inspire others. Apply the principles of hypnosis so that you can motivate others to work on your behalf. Instill a spirit of pride and loyalty in those who are working for you or under you. The following ideas will enable you to do this:

  1. Stress their personal importance to you and to your organization.

2. Stress the importance of their work. Never refer to their work as a job, but as a position, skill, or trade.
3. Identify them with your firm or organization in every way possible.
4. Point out their errors in private. Praise them in public.
5. Give them constant incentives to do more.
6. Use training programs which place the emphasis on positive suggestion and personal growth. If possible, use hypnosis.
7. Recognize the worth and value of the employee's family.
8. Give incentives to the wife so that she will motivate her husband. Instead of offering a yearly bonus for a certain amount of production, offer a family vacation. Instead of giving the salesman a new suit for reaching a particular sales plateau, give both the husband and wife a new outfit.
9. Be positive and cheerful yourself. A good attitude is contagious, so is a bad one.
10. Be firm without being nasty.

The right kind of motivation can save you a great amount of money and lost labor.

14. Make God your partner in all your endeavors. Don't divide your life into spiritual and secular categories. God is just as interested in your temporal well-being as He is in your spiritual well-being. He makes a wonderful business partner. So:

1. Acknowledge His presence at all times.
2. Engage in daily prayer.
3. Seek His guidance.
4. Give generously to your church or some worthy charity. I have done this all my life, and I have never missed the money. It will create a generous spirit within you and protect you from greed. It will make you aware of the needs of others. Don't do this unless you are really sold on it. God doesn't need your money, but you do need God's blessing.

15. Accept success when it comes your way. I have left this point until last, but it is one of the most important. Many work for years to attain success, and when it finally arrives they don't know what to do with it. It scares them to death. Preparation for success is very important. Some people feel unworthy or inadequate for the prestige and responsibilities which are linked with success. I have known instances where people let others reap the fruits of their labors. Others "blow" in a short time their years of effort.

Acting like a success before you become a success will help to prepare you psychologically for the day when your star arises. Another aid in accepting and maintaining success is not to change your living and spending habits overnight. Above all, feel you are worthy of success. Feel that God has given you success. Accept it as a beneficent gift from the Giver of every good and perfect gift.

Think success, live success, and you will be a success!

SELF-HYPNOSIS SUGGESTION FOR FINANCIAL SUCCESS

Because (insert your own P.D.E.M.) financial success is coming to me day by day. I automatically practice the principles of success. I am a success in every phase of my life.

HIGHLIGHTS TO REMEMBER FROM THIS CHAPTER:

1. Know where you are going.
2. Give yourself the proper P.D.E.M. for reaching your goal in life.
3. Give yourself adequate preparation.
4. You must have determination.
5. You must have self-confidence.
6. Think big!
7. You must be capable of making decisions.
8. Harness the power of your imagination.
9. You must be willing to work hard.
10. You must take care of your problems as they arise.
11. You must not be governed by circumstances. You make your own circumstances.
12. Don't be afraid to make mistakes.
13. You must be able to motivate others.
14. Make God your partner.
15. Accept success when it comes.
16. A self-hypnosis suggestion is given for financial success.

16

HOW SELF-HYPNOSIS
CAN HELP YOU CONTROL
YOUR EMOTIONS

ANGER, DEPRESSION, FEAR, ANXIETY, AND guilt are your worst enemies. These are emotions or states of mind which can literally tear you apart. These negative emotions have an adverse effect on you physically, mentally, and spiritually. They can rack the body and crack the mind. When these emotions are exacerbated they create a spiritual emptiness.

Few people know how to deal effectively with their emotions. Either they are constantly repressing them, or else they are always "blowing their stacks." The latter behavior exemplifies a modern fallacy: If you blow your stack and let off your steam you will never have any emotional problems. This is false. Many of my sickest clients are people who are always blowing their stacks. These people do have severe emotional problems. Blowing their stack only helps to create more problems for them. By the way, they usually don't have too many friends.

It is good emotionally to let off your steam a little bit at a time. You should control the release of this emotional steam. There is a vast difference between controlled releasing of steam and a complete blow-up. The person who never represses an emotion is just as sick, if not sicker, than the individual who represses all his feelings.

Repression, withdrawal, projection, rationalization, and hostility are all normal human defense patterns, which can be used to cope with negative emotions. They become abnormal when they are carried to excess. If you were to repress all distasteful, hurtful experiences it wouldn't be long until you would be in a very dangerous emotional state. Yet there are times when it will be expedient and beneficial for you to repress certain bad experiences. It is the emotionally mature individual who knows when and how to use repression.

We all project our hurts and faults to others at times. We are all given to rationalizations on occasion. Everyone withdraws to a degree at some time or another. Everyone has his moments of hostility. This is natural. It's an indication you are alive. When one or more of these defense mechanisms become constant and excessive in your life then it is time to remedy the situation. Self-hypnosis can help you keep your natural defenses in good working order and at the same time help you become the master of your emotions.

ANXIETY A TORMENTOR

Anxiety has always been a tormentor of man. The individual afflicted with this terrible mental and spiritual disease is the most miserable of all men. He worries about things for which he has no rational basis for worry. He is afraid he is going to lose his job, despite the fact he is doing excellent work and his employer is well pleased with him. His body is as sound as a dollar, but he is sure he has heart trouble or cancer. Even though his children are ideal, he worries that they might become criminals, dope-addicts, or prostitutes. Earthquakes, tornadoes, war, and depression are all imminent. These things are all possibilities, but to sit around and wait for them to happen is utter nonsense.

Fear of an atomic war causes more anxiety in modern man than anything else. This of course is a definite possibility, but worrying about it doesn't help. I hope and pray it will never happen, but I don't worry about it. If it does occur and the bomb hits near me, I won't know anything about it. It will be a quick way to die.

HOW A CASE OF ANXIETY WAS HANDLED

I recently counseled a gentleman who was in a constant state of anxiety about his wife and daughter. He said he loved them so much he was afraid something tragic was going to happen to them. His condition became so serious that he was afraid to go to work because something might happen while he wasn't there to protect them. This behavior naturally had a detrimental effect upon his work, his marriage, and his total relationship with his fellowmen.

After a few counseling sessions, I discovered that at an early age this man had lost everything he loved in life. With hypnotic age regression I learned of an incident at the age of six which seemed to precipitate his anxiety state. He had a dog to which he had a strong attachment. One day the dog got loose and was killed by a passing truck. When he was fifteen his father died. With his father's death his hopes for college also died. At the age of nineteen his mother died. Both parents died as a result of accidents. His father was killed at work, and his mother was killed in an automobile accident.

As a result he was convinced subconsciously that anything he loved would be lost to him. Hypnosis and self-hypnosis were used to convince him that all was well, and that he didn't have to engage in useless worry.

Here are some pointers which can help you live without anxiety controlling your life.

One, realize that God loves you. He wants to be your Father. He will keep you and sustain you if you will trust Him.

Two, ask yourself this question: "What is the worst thing that can happen to me if what I fear happens to me?" Think the situation through to its most extreme eventuality. Would you lose your job, your home, your wife, your children? Would you die? All of these things would be terrible, but you could survive. That is, you could survive all but death. If you die you go to be with God. The human being is capable of tremendous adjustment. If you were to lose your house as a result of a depression the majority of your friends and neighbors would be in the same predicament. Most of the houses would revert to the government, and the government would probably rent your house back to you. It could be worse, couldn't it?

Three, put into practice everything you have learned about faith. Develop a positive, limited, realistic, active belief. Extend it in all five of its directions. Believe in God, in yourself, in your fellowman. Believe in the past and in the future. If you learn to live by and in faith, you will be rid of most anxiety.

Four, give yourself a strong P.D.E.M. for overcoming your anxieties. Tell yourself that the happiness of yourself and your loved ones mean more to you than a meaningless anxiety. You can't do your best at anything when you are nursing an anxiety.

Five, live a day at a time. This advice isn't original, but it is good counsel; and it will work if you will work it. Keep your life-goals in mind, but live one day at a time. Our Lord said, "Take therefore no thought for the morrow; for the morrow shall take thought for the things of itself. Sufficient unto the day is the evil thereof." (Mat. 6:34 K.J.V.)

If you take care of today's problems today, you will have no difficulty in handling tomorrow's problems. Expend all your energies in living today, and you won't have time worrying about tomorrow.

Six, realize that most of the things you worry about will never happen. It is a useless waste of emotion. Even if something does happen, being anxious about it certainly won't help.

Seven, use self-hypnosis to overcome anxiety. Feed yourself positive suggestions which will help you overcome anxieties.

SELF-HYPNOSIS SUGGESTION
TO OVERCOME ANXIETY

Because (insert your own *P.D.E.M.*) I have great faith in all five of its aspects. I especially believe that I can cope with anything which might happen in my life. The goodness, mercy, and grace of God are always with me. I expend all my energies in living one day at a time.

Fear is to be distinguished from anxiety. In anxiety the individual has no realistic basis for his worries. Fear is an emotional response to a given set of circumstances. For example, a man is confronted with a mad dog, and he reacts with fear. There is no logical reason for anxiety, but there is for fear. It is normal to be fearful at times. There isn't a human living who isn't fearful once in a while. Fear becomes abnormal when it is carried to excess.

You would be a fool if you didn't have a healthy amount of fear in regard to fire and other dangerous forces which you encounter in life. Normal fear is an emotion which God has given us to keep us from needless harm and death. If your fear of fire became so extreme that it hindered your normal living processes, then your fear would be abnormal. In fact, I would no longer call it fear, but I would designate it as an anxiety.

One of the best explanations of fear is found in the way the word "fear" is used in the Scriptures. Proverbs 1:7 K.J.V. states: "The fear of the Lord is the beginning of knowledge . . ." Some believe this Scripture means you should be afraid of God. But they are completely mistaken. It literally means we should have a "reverential trust" in God.

If we were to put the expression in our everyday speech we would say: "The *reverence* of the Lord" or "The *respect* of the Lord . . ." When you revere something you *respect* it. This "right kind of fear" is the beginning of knowledge, or a knowledge of God creates a reverence and respect for the Lord. This is the beginning of all knowledge. If you apply this to the truths concerning faith (refer to Chapter 11) you will understand the effect this can have upon your life. If you are *afraid* of God, you will be afraid of yourself, your fellowman, your past, and your future. If you *revere* and *respect* God, you will revere and respect yourself, your fellowman, your past, and your future.

When I was five years of age, our family moved into a house my father was building by himself. It was far from completed. The outside was covered with tar-paper. Inside there were bare two-by-fours which indicated where the rooms would eventually be. In the midst of all these two-by-fours was an old fashioned, pot-bellied stove. When the stove was loaded with coal or wood it would become red hot. My mother and grandmother repeatedly warned me not to get too close to the stove. Despite all their solemn admonitions, I burned the backside of my anatomy one day while trying to keep warm. From that moment on, I had respect for that stove. I never got too close again. But I didn't allow this experience to keep me from using it in the proper manner. I still hovered near the stove to warm myself after I was thoroughly chilled from playing outside. I respected the stove, but I wasn't afraid of it.

One of my favorite Scriptures is II Timothy K.J.V.; "For God hath not given us the spirit of *fear;* but of power, and of love, and of a sound mind." The word "fear" here means an abject fear. It means to fear something when there is no need of fear. A better word might be the word anxiety—fearing something when there is no real basis for fear. Another modern psychological word which could be used here is the word "phobia." Modern man has all sorts of phobias—acrophobia (fear of heights), claustrophobia (fear of closed-in spaces), agoraphobia (fear of open spaces), plus others ad infinitum. People are afraid of other people. They are afraid of sickness, the loss of their job, of life, and death.

This type of fear which we today would classify as anxiety or phobia *does not come from God.* The "beginning of knowledge," reverence and respect for God and ourselves comes from God. Commonsense respect for dangerous and harmful objects and situations comes from God.

OVERCOMING USELESS FEARS

Here are some pointers which will help you to overcome useless fears and help you to use normal fear as a constructive force.

1. Determine whether or not you have a realistic basis for your fears. Is there a real reason for you to be fearful, or would your fear be classified as an anxiety or phobia?

2. Begin to think of fear in the sense of "having respect for," instead of "being afraid of." If you have an enemy you should respect his power and capabilities, but you shouldn't be afraid of him.

3. Once you fully understand point two, begin to use and control your fears to your advantage and benefit. The Bible gives us a wonderful example of how this can be done. "By faith Noah, being warned of God of things not seen as yet moved with fear, prepared an ark to the saving of his house . . ." (Heb. 11:7 K.J.V.) Notice the words, "Noah . . . *moved with fear.*" Instead of allowing his fear to paralyze or destroy him, he used it

as a positive force. His fear made him work harder, faster and more effectively. A good public speaker always has a slight case of "nerves," but he utilizes this nervous energy, generated by fear, to be dynamic and forceful in his speaking. He has respect for his audience, and he knows what can happen to him if he fails. This knowledge is used to his advantage.

4. Acknowledge to yourself that needless, baseless fear does not come from God. This is an emotion which is foreign to God.

5. Live each day and each moment with the awareness of God's presence.

6. Give yourself a strong P.D.E.M. and a realistic goal which will help you live a life without fear.

7. Constantly strive to strengthen your faith. Faith and fear cannot live together.

8. Use self-hypnosis to help you accomplish the elimination of useless fears from your life.

SELF-HYPNOSIS SUGGESTION TO ELIMINATE USELESS FEAR

Because (insert your own *P.D.E.M.*) I have respect for all things, but I am afraid of nothing.

OVERCOMING THE EMOTION OF GUILT

Excessive guilt is an emotion which can cause much damage to your personality and your life. Guilt, like fear (respect based on knowledge), is a necessary component of man's personality. Fear keeps us from harm. Guilt keeps us from harming others. When we perform an act which brings harm to our fellowman, we should feel a sense of compunction which will motivate us to rectify the wrong. I believe all right thinking people would be in agreement on this point. Intent should be considered when we accept the guilt or blame for an act or deed. Ask yourself, "Did I deliberately intend to harm this person, or did I harm him accidentally?" When you have done wrong you should acknowledge it and as much as possible correct the wrong.

I have found that numerous people go through life with a false sense of guilt. They are constantly condemning themselves for things for which they are not responsible. It is very common for people to entertain a false guilt in regard to the death of a loved one. A young mother once told me she had not slept well for two years, and she thought she would never sleep again, because she felt responsible for the death of her two-month old baby. Her feeling of guilt was completely unfounded. She had stayed with the child day and night during its illness. In fact, she almost ruined her health caring for the sick baby, for it had been dead two years, and the mother was still in poor health. Another reason why she had no need to feel guilty was that the baby would have died no matter what had or had not been done for it. It was an illness for which medical science doesn't as yet have a cure. Despite all this, the young mother felt guilty. Counseling, prayer, and hypnosis enabled me to change her thinking and rid her of this useless guilt.

Some people feel guilty about spending money, enjoying life and sex. There are people who feel guilty about everything. Much of the blame can be placed on religion. The Scriptures and commonsense teach us the world was made by God for man's benefit and enjoyment. Everything in this would can be used by man in the proper manner and with moderation. When he lives with this knowledge, he doesn't have to live with guilt. Before you begin to blame yourself for something, ask yourself, "Was this really wrong? If so, what makes it wrong?"

God and the Bible get blamed for many false ideas. Somebody will say, "You shouldn't do that, it's sinful." You might reply, "Oh is that so? Where do you find in the Bible that this is sinful?" Invariably, they don't know where to find it in the Bible, but they know it is there. Yet you could search for a thousand years and never find a word concerning it in the Bible.

False feelings of guilt concerning sex have ruined countless lives and marriages. Some, who have worked hard for years, cannot enjoy their wealth because of a false feeling of guilt in regard to their own money.

HOW TO FORGIVE YOURSELF

A situation I have encountered quite often is where an individual has done a real or an imagined wrong and will ask and accept God's forgiveness, but will not forgive himself. "I just can't forgive myself. I have done this terrible thing, and I will never be able to forget it." When someone has this attitude it is quite evident he hasn't completely accepted God's forgiveness. If he really believed God had forgiven him, he would forgive himself. The Scriptures state, "If we confess our sins, He is faithful and just to forgive us our sins, and to cleanse us from all unrighteousness." (I John 1:9 K.J.V.) When we ask God for forgiveness He forgives. No matter what the sin is, He forgives. No matter how often we ask, He forgives. It is imperative therefore that we accept His forgiveness and also forgive ourselves.

Feelings of guilt come from our early training and conditioning. It is most important that parents do not inflict false feelings of guilt in the superegos of their children. Be careful of the impressions you make on the minds of your little ones.

Here are some pointers to help rid your life of false guilt.

One, determine whether your feeling of guilt is real or false. Did you really do something wrong and harmful to your fellowman? Did you do it intentionally or accidentally?

Two, if you have intentionally done wrong, ask for and accept God's forgiveness. Ask the forgiveness of the one harmed, if this is possible. Forgive yourself.

Three, examine your ideas and concepts as to what is right or wrong. Perhaps you are living a limited life because of erroneous ideas. If you have doubts, seek out a minister or psychologist for advice.

Four, use self-hypnosis to rid yourself of all false guilt. Forget the past and live today.

SELF-HYPNOSIS SUGGESTION TO DO AWAY WITH FALSE GUILT

Because (insert your own *P.D.E.M.*) I acknowledge and seek forgiveness for all real wrongs I have committed. I accept God's forgiveness and I forgive myself. I am free of all false guilt and blame. This world was made for my benefit and enjoyment; therefore, I enjoy all of it.

OVERCOMING DEPRESSION

We all become somewhat depressed at times. Everyone has his blue Mondays, or it might be blue Wednesdays. Personally, the worst day of my week, if I happen to have a bad day, is Friday. Please don't ask me why, or say, "Physician heal thyself." I don't know why this is. It is just one of those things I have accepted. Like all other emotions it is normal for you to have "the blues" once in a while. The individual who says he is never depressed is either lying or else he is very sick.

Extreme depression is a very dangerous condition. The manic-depressive state is almost certain death, unless the individual suffering from it receives immediate attention. If this condition is left unchecked, the sufferer will end his misery with suicide. Extreme or endogenous depression is depression which comes from within the person. A change of circumstance affects the depression very little. This type of depression is also very intense and prolonged. Once again, I stress the fact that this is a very dangerous condition and warrants immediate psychiatric attention. When someone comes into my office and expresses symptoms which indicate extreme endogenous depression, I immediately refer them for psychiatric attention. *Do not try to cure this condition or any other severe condition with self-hypnosis or any other form of self-cure!* Seek professional help.

Now that I have scared you half to death, let us consider the kinds of depression self-hypnosis can help. Self-hypnosis is very beneficial in combating mild depressive states. Most normal depressive conditions are caused by circumstances. There is usually a set of factors which correlate to trigger off the depression. Many times understanding what these factors are brings total or partial relief from the depression. If you are able to discern the cause or causes of your depression, stay away from it or them as much as possible. Better yet, change your attitude toward the cause of your depressive mood. You don't have to be depressed unless you want to be depressed. Begin to react with an attitude of rejoicing instead of an attitude of depression.

One of my clients was feeling very depressed over the dull routine of his life. He was twenty-five, married, and the father of two young children. At the time he sought my help, he was working in one of the local automobile factories at night and carrying a full load of studies at college during the day. All he did was work and go to school. His wife was more than understanding, but he was beginning to feel guilty, because he neglected her and the children. Part of his problem was lack of proper rest and diet, but beyond this it was a matter of attitude. In the midst of all his intense efforts, he had forgotten what his goals were and why he was in school. Things were rough, but his wife knew they were both making sacrifices, so they and their children might enjoy a better life in the future. I worked with this young man in three areas. I taught him self-hypnosis so he might learn to relax more effectively. He was also taught how to use self-hypnosis to increase his powers of concentration and memory. At the same time I reaffirmed his goals and desires for the future while in hypnosis.

Here are some pointers which will help counteract depression in your life.

1. Determine, as much as possible, the circumstances which caused your depression.

2. Change your attitude toward these factors.

3. Ask yourself whether or not you enjoy your depression. Do you enjoy feeling sorry for yourself?

4. Add as much variety as you can to your life. Avoid boredom.

5. Mingle with people as often as you can. It is quite difficult to remain depressed if you are with happy people.

6. Practice positive faith in all five directions.

7. Learn to love life. Start to live.

8. Give yourself a strong P.D.E.M. for being happy.

9. Give yourself the goal of being joyous.

10. Think of all the blessings which God has bestowed upon you.

11. Thank God, in prayer, for these blessings.

12. Use self-hypnosis to feed your subconscious with thoughts of happiness and joy.

SELF-HYPNOSIS SUGGESTION TO RID YOURSELF OF DEPRESSION

Because (insert your own *P.D.E.M.*) I am happy at all times and under all circumstances. God's goodness and grace is with me. I rejoice in times of adversity as well as in times of joy. My happiness is from within and is not dependent on outward circumstances.

CONTROLLING TEMPER

"I just can't hold my temper," is a complaint I hear from a number of frustrated people. I know this sounds a little repetitious, but I mention it because of its importance. The emotion of anger is normal. If you don't ever get angry, you are either sick or dead. The important thing is that you master your anger instead of allowing your anger to master you. The Apostle Paul says that it is possible to be angry without sinning. "Be ye angry, and sin not; let not the sun go down upon your wrath." (Eph. 4:26 K.J.V.)

It is possible to control your temper. My grandfather used to tell me that the bully who could never hold his temper usually managed to calm down when someone tougher than he was around. You can master your hostilities if you really want to.

Here are a few pointers which will help you overcome hostilities.

1. Try to ascertain the cause of your hostility. Why do certain things and certain people irritate you? Is it because of an unpleasant situation from your past? Do you have a legitimate reason to be upset? Are you angry with yourself?

2. Don't harbour bitterness and resentment in your heart. If you do, you will harm yourself more than anyone else. Bitter, hostile people are never happy people. They are usually friendless and lonely. Stop thinking about the hurts of the past. Reliving bad experiences only serves to keep them alive. Mr. Lincoln was asked by a friend why he didn't answer his critics and defend himself. President Lincoln said he was too busy with important things and didn't have time for pettiness.

3. Give the other fellow the benefit of the doubt. Did he deliberately make that remark to offend you, or are you taking offence without just reason?

4. Learn to overlook the ignorance of some people. Consider the source of derogatory statements. Don't please such people by responding to their stupidity.

5. Practice forgiving and forgetting. To do this completely is humanly impossible, but any degree of success in this matter will add real depth and maturity to your character.

6. Act, don't react to any given situation. Evaluate each per-

son or incident on the basis of who they are or what it is. Give yourself time to think before you blow your lid.

7. Give yourself the goal of having a peaceful nature.
8. Give yourself a strong P.D.E.M. for accomplishing your goal.
9. Reinforce all this with self-hypnosis.

SELF-HYPNOSIS SUGGESTION TO HELP YOU OVERCOME YOUR HOSTILITIES

Because (insert your own *P.D.E.M.*) I am at peace with God, with myself and with my fellowman.

HIGHLIGHTS TO REMEMBER FROM THIS CHAPTER:

1. Negative, excessive emotions are your worst enemies.
2. Blowing your stack doesn't solve your emotional problems.
3. Repression, withdrawal, projection, etc. are normal defense mechanisms which can be used to help us cope with negative emotions. They become abnormal when carried to excess.
4. Anxiety is a state wherein the individual worries about matters for which there is no rational basis for worry.
5. Seven pointers which will help you overcome your anxieties are given.
6. Fear is different from anxiety.
7. Fear is an emotional response to a given set of circumstances.
8. The "fear of the Lord" means a respect for the Lord. An understanding of God creates respect or reverence for God.
9. Abject fear doesn't come from God.
10. Eight pointers which will help you overcome useless fears are given.
11. Guilt is a normal emotion which keeps us from harming others.
12. Excessive guilt can do great harm.
13. False guilt can ruin your life.
14. Four pointers to rid your life of false guilt are given.
15. Mild depression is normal. Extreme, intense, chronic depression is very dangerous.
16. Twelve pointers to help you overcome depression are given.
17. Anger is normal if it is not carried to excess.
18. Nine pointers to help you overcome your hostilities are given.
19. Self-hypnosis suggestions are given for overcoming anxiety, fear, guilt, depression, and hostility.

17

HOW SELF-HYPNOSIS CAN HELP YOU IMPROVE YOUR POWERS OF CONCENTRATION AND MEMORY

WE CALL THE TIME IN which we live the space age. Another term which might be more descriptive would be the mind age. Both of these designations have a direct application to the more progressive nations of the world. Man is moving very rapidly into outer space. More men today are earning their daily bread with their brains than with their brawn.

I overheard a conversation the other day between a grandfather and his ten-year old grandson. The grandfather was reminiscing to his grandson in a boastful way. He was pointing out how soft and weak this modern generation is. "Son, when I was your age I was doing a man's work. I was plowing behind two mares all day long. . . ." His grandson replied, "That's true, Grandpa, but did you have to learn modern math, Spanish, biology, etc. when you were in the fourth grade?" This little story illustrates the nature of the age in which we live. Most space age citizens are earning their bread by the "sweat of their minds."

TAPPING THE POWER OF THE SUBCONSCIOUS

Not many of us are genuises; therefore, we must learn to use the mind-power we have to its fullest potential. Above all, we must learn to tap the great reservoir of power which resides in the subconscious. Hypnosis and self-hypnosis can enable you to accomplish the almost unbelievable in the areas of concentration and memory. The reasonableness of this statement is demonstrated by the fact that the states of hypnosis and concentration are blood brothers. When your mind is fully concentrated on a book, T.V., etc., you are in hypnosis. Likewise, when you are in hypnosis, you are in a state of hyper-concentration. The subconscious is the eventual storehouse of all memories; because of this the memory is also closely associated with hypnosis.

IMPORTANCE OF GOOD STUDY HABITS

Before proceeding further, I would like to mention something which is very important. Not even hypnosis or self-hypnosis can take the place of good study habits. A number of students come to me for help with their studies with the erroneous idea that if they learn self-hypnosis they will not have to study any more. This idea is, of course, completely wrong. Hypnosis cannot put mind-power in you, but it can help you use the mind-power you have. You can become an expert at self-hypnosis, but if you don't apply this ability to your studies it certainly isn't going to benefit you. The individual who thinks it will is like the uneducated minister who always bragged about his lack of learning. He said he never studied for sermons. All he had to do, when he preached, was open his mouth and the Lord filled it. One of his parishioners said, "Yeah, your mouth gets filled all right. It gets filled with hot air."

There are many books and courses dealing with study habits, so we won't dwell on the subject any further. If you are deficient in this area, take the ideas from one of these books or from one of your instructors and write a self-hypnosis formula, and feed it to your subconscious. It won't be long until you will develop constructive study habits.

Do not be deceived into believing you were born with a poor

memory or with a faulty ability to concentrate. Anyone with an average I.Q. can learn how to concentrate and can develop a powerful memory. The difference between the individual who concentrates well and remembers well, and the individual who does both poorly, is that one has trained his mind and the other hasn't. If you lack these capabilities, start today to acquire them. Utilize your imagination, plus the hypnotic techniques given in this chapter to enhance and improve the power of your mind.

If you possess an average I.Q., you can achieve a grade average somewhere between a "C+" and a "B" if you will diligently use self-hypnosis. If your I.Q. is well above average, you, of course, can do much better, depending on your efforts.

Some people do poorly in school or in a particular subject, because they have been convinced subconsciously they are dumb. Somewhere along the line someone has done an excellent job of brainwashing them into believing they are stupid. When these unfortunate people are motivated in the proper manner, they are able to do what they previously thought impossible.

I encountered a situation a few months ago which vividly illustrates this truth. A mother brought her fourteen-year old son to me for help with his school work. She told me he was basically dumb, but she hoped I might be able to do him some good. "Too bad," she said, "that he isn't a brain like his older sister. She's an all "A" student." When I heard this, I knew I wouldn't have to search too far for the cause of the problem. I was right. Through the years this young man had lived in the shadow of his sister's scholastic acumen. He had constantly been bombarded with the suggestion that he was as dumb as his sister was smart. As a result, he accepted himself as slow and stupid. Therefore, he made no real effort to study. No matter what he might have done, it wouldn't have been good enough. I convinced this boy subconsciously that he could get good marks, and that he could do well in school. The parents were also advised to stop comparing their son with his sister. Instead they were to encourage and reassure him. Since that time this young man has done average or above average work in school.

NO SUCH THING AS A SPECIAL TYPE BRAIN

Believe it or not, there isn't any such thing as a "mechanical brain" or a "mathematical brain" or a "business brain," etc. Children are told they can't possibly do well in a subject because they haven't got a certain type of brain or mind. The individual who relates this information to them is usually an authority figure of some kind. The suggestion quite often has a lasting effect upon the child. I realize that different people have different aptitudes for different things. It is also true that a few people do have "learning blocks" in regard to certain subjects, but their percentage is small. The people I am talking about, however, are normal people with normal aptitudes. They have brains. They do not have "math brains," "mechanical brains," "grammar brains," etc. If they can do well in one subject, they can do relatively well in every other subject unless they are convinced otherwise.

HYPNOSIS FOR BETTER LEARNING

Now that we have cleared away some fallacies about learning and about assorted "brains," let us see how self-hypnosis can help to develop greater capacities for learning. There are three areas where you can use self-hypnosis to improve your scholastic abilities: in your ability to concentrate, your ability to recall and remember, and to make you calm and relaxed while taking examinations.

My approach to these study abilities is to instill motivation in the student, and at the same time teach him hypnotic techniques which will facilitate his skills.

Motivation is of tremendous importance. If you enjoy studying a certain subject, you have no difficulty in concentrating on it. If you concentrate well on a subject, you find it easy to comprehend the subject matter. If you comprehend the subject matter, you find it easy to recall and remember it when you wish. Conversely, if you don't like a subject, it is hard for you to really concentrate on it. Because of this you have difficulty in comprehending the material, and you also can't recall or remember very easily. The thing you have to work on then is to find a P.D.E.M. which will give you the proper incentive to make you want to learn and enjoy this subject.

George Jones was a young pre-med student who was having difficulty with chemistry. He didn't like chemistry. In fact, he had never cared for chemistry. To him it was dry and boring. It was this attitude which kept him from doing his best in the subject. After conversing with him for a while, I asked him why he wanted to be a physician, and how important was it to him to get his M.D. His reply was that he wanted to be a doctor because he felt it was a means of rendering a valuable service to mankind. Becoming a physician meant more to him than anything else in the world. It was important to him also because his parents were uneducated people, and they were extremely proud of him and his academic accomplishments. After teaching George the fundamentals of self-hypnosis, we wrote a suggestion which solved his difficulties in chemistry. His P.D.E.M. was that his great desire to be a physician and the approval of his parents made him take a real interest in chemistry, because a knowledge of chemistry was essential to his profession.

When I deal with people in high school, I become elementary in determining their P.D.E.M.s. I get them to talk about what they want to be in life and about what they want in life. Eventually they get around to telling me about the high-powered sports car they want to own some day. Or perhaps it might be a beautiful home or expensive clothing or an exotic vacation. . . . Then I ask if they have any conception as to the cost of these items. Sometimes they do; sometimes they don't. Once we establish a cost, I then ask how long they would have to work and save before they would have enough money to pay for the commodity they desire. At this point, I proceed to tell them the amount of education they acquire will determine the amount of money they will earn during their lifetime. If they want a good life in the future, they had better get all the education possible today. Cars, houses, clothes, and vacation trips cost money. Good paying positions go to those who are trained for them. This type of motivation has proved very effective in keeping young people in school.

The same approach can be used for the students who are having trouble with a particular subject. If they want to go to college and own that sports car, etc., they will have to get through high school and they will have to pass this subject. Because they have a burning desire to own their own sports car or whatever their P.D.E.M. might be, they will become more interested in math, English, etc. Some of these P.D.E.M.s might not seem too worthy to the mature adults, but these are the emotional mainsprings which motivate young people. Therefore, use them in a positive manner to guide the youth in the right direction. The career as a movie actress or the hot rod car are no doubt passing fancies in the lives of the average teenager, but they are very real to them at the moment they desire them. Don't try to change their ideas, but use their ideas as a positive constructive force. As they mature, their ideas will automatically change. The important thing is that you motivate them to stay in school and improve their marks and study habits.

Another way of instilling motivation into yourself or your child to take interest in a subject which is unappealing, is to stress the fact that knowledge is power. All humans have the innate desire to be affluent and powerful. The more you learn the more powerful you become. The men and women on top of the heap today are not people who are strong physically, but people who are strong mentally.

The desire to help others is an altruistic motivation which is very effective with some individuals. The more you learn, including subjects you don't like, the better equipped you will be to serve God and man.

Another method which works well is to show how the uninteresting subject is related to subjects which the student finds interesting. Emphasize the relationship between the subjects and ignore the difficulties.

Interest can also be created in a subject by relating it in a practical way to your daily living. Math, grammar, etc. would all be very dry if you didn't use these areas of learning in your everyday life. Quite often a student will ask, "Why do I have to learn this?" If you can give him a reasonable answer, you have won half the battle.

HYPNOTISM FOR BETTER CONCENTRATION, COMPREHENSION, AND MEMORY

Now that we have dealt with motivation to study, let us move on to hypnotic techniques which will improve your powers of concentration, comprehension, and memory. One simple and yet quite often effective method is to give yourself the suggestion, while in hypnosis, that you will concentrate and comprehend fully and completely when you study. You will also be able to recall and remember, at will, everything you have learned. Each day your ability to concentrate, comprehend, and remember increases. This simple suggestion has changed the lives and the self-image of many people.

I appeal a great deal to the imagination when trying to improve the learning abilities of students. Here are four images you can use to improve your concentration and memory: a sponge, a camera, a tape recorder, and an electronic computer. Hypnotize yourself and use one of the following suggestions. Try them all first. Then use the one which is most effective with you.

SELF-HYPNOSIS SUGGESTIONS FOR IMPROVING CONCENTRATION AND MEMORY
THE SPONGE

My mind is like a huge sponge which automatically absorbs knowledge. Everything I read, hear, see, or experience is absorbed by my mind. Everything I absorb I retain. All the material I learn is stored permanently in my subconscious and is available to me at all times. I can recall and remember anything I wish at any time by merely saying the word *squeeze*. When I say *squeeze*, that which I want to remember comes out of my mind as water comes out of a sponge.

THE CAMERA

My mind is like a camera. Everything I read, hear, see, or experience is photographed by my mind. My mind is able to photograph words, sentences, paragraphs, and pages of books, magazines, and newspapers. My mind photographs everything it sees. Everything my mind photographs it permanently retains, and I can recall and remember names, places, dates, books, faces, numbers, and data of any kind whenever I wish.

Whenever I begin to study I say to myself—focus, focus, focus —and I go into a complete state of concentration until I am finished with my work. Everything that I fully concentrate upon I am able to completely comprehend. Everything I completely comprehend, I am able to remember.

THE TAPE RECORDER

My mind is like a tape recorder. Everything I hear, see, or experience is recorded in my mind. Everything my mind records it retains. I have a permanent record in my mind of everything

I read, see, hear, or experience. I am able to recall and remember names, places, dates, books, lectures, faces, and data of any kind when I wish. All I have to do to remember anything is to send a message to my subconscious as to what I wish to remember. Then I say—playback, playback, playback—and in a few minutes the answer comes to me.

Whenever I begin to study I say to myself—tune in, tune in, tune in—and I go into a complete state of concentration until I am finished with my work. Everything I fully concentrate upon I am able to completely comprehend. Everything I completely comprehend I am able to remember.

THE ELECTRONIC COMPUTER

My mind is like an electronic computer. I feed data into it by reading and listening. Everything which is fed into it is thoroughly and properly evaluated. The data is associated with and related to all previous knowledge stored in my mind. Everything fed into my computer is permanently retained and is available to me at all times. Whenever I wish to recall and remember anything, I merely say the words—push, push, push—and it is immediately available to me.

These suggestions are somewhat longer than most of the suggestions in this book, but I have found them to be very effective. Because they are rather lengthy, I have omitted the P.D.E.M. You may insert your P.D.E.M. at the beginning of the suggestion by saying: Because *P.D.E.M.* my mind . . .

I have used these four mental images because they have worked well with my students, but I am sure you can think of other images which will work as well or better with you.

OVERCOMING EXAMINATION AND CRISIS "FREEZE"

Examination freeze is a common malady among students. They have studied the subject matter; they know it; but when they face the examination, they freeze. It is impossible for them to think accurately. Their memory and power of recall leaves them. Many times a worthy student will fail a course, or receive a very inferior mark, because of this situation.

About two years ago, I worked with a young man who had this

problem. He always did well with his daily assignments, but usually failed his semester exams because of tension. When he came to me he was on probation. If he didn't raise his marks considerably, he would be dropped from school. He was in his junior year at a local college and wanted very much to finish school. At first I saw him twice a week for three weeks. Then once a week for three weeks. Finally, I saw him only every other week until school was out. When he received his marks, he was so jubilant he called and told me he had received the best grades of his college career. This experience gave him enough confidence so that he no longer needed my personal attention, but he still uses self-hypnosis as an intrinsic part of his study procedure.

When confronted with the problem of examination freeze, you should analyze yourself as much as you can to determine why you freeze. Are you afraid of authority figures which the teacher represents? Are you afraid of competition? Are you afraid of the unknown? Are you afraid of failure? These are just a few of the questions you should ask yourself. Once you have made this determination, deal with the problem. Form a suggestion and feed it into the subconscious through self-hypnosis.

It is not uncommon for a student to experience examination freeze in one class and not in another. The reason is usually a fear of the instructor or fear of the subject. Consciously the student will deny this, but subconsciously it is true.

Let me ask you a question. When you are driving your automobile and are faced with a crisis situation, how do you react? Do you panic and freeze up? If you did this very often you wouldn't be here to answer my question. Normally, your subconscious would entirely take over the situation. Your response would be automatic and precise. Your coordination and timing would be perfect. You would react in a manner *far superior* to your normal response patterns. Instead of freezing or falling apart, you allow the tremendous power of your subconscious to take full command of the situation. You can do the same thing during every crisis situation of your life, including your examinations. Don't freeze up. Allow your subconscious to take full command and see you successfully through your examinations. Give yourself the following suggestion to overcome examination freeze.

SELF-HYPNOSIS SUGGESTION TO OVERCOME EXAMINATION FREEZE

Because (*P.D.E.M.*—insert your own) I am completely calm, confident, and relaxed when taking my examination. I react in a positive manner similar to the way I respond when faced with a crisis situation while driving my car. My mind acts with complete accuracy and delivers the right answer to every question. All knowledge is completely available to me. I write the best examination paper possible.

Here are some pointers which will help you improve your ability to learn and remember.

1. Give yourself the goal of getting good marks.
2. Give yourself a strong P.D.E.M. to help you achieve this goal.
3. Believe in yourself and your ability to achieve good marks.
4. Analyze and deal with any special learning problems you might have.
5. Develop and maintain good study habits.
6. Use the self-hypnosis suggestions found in this chapter until they are a part of you.

HIGHLIGHTS TO REMEMBER FROM THIS CHAPTER:

1. This is the "mind-age." Most people make their living with their brain, not their brawn.
2. The state of hypnosis and concentration of the mind are closely related.
3. Self-hypnosis isn't a substitute for good study habits.
4. People are not born with poor memories and bad powers of concentration.
5. Some people do poorly in school because they have been subconsciously convinced that they are stupid.
6. You do not have a "mechanical brain," etc. You merely have a brain. If you do well in one subject, you can do well in all subjects.
7. Self-hypnosis can improve your powers of concentration and memory and can help you be calm and confident during examinations.

8. Motivation is the key to increasing concentration, comprehension, and the ability to remember a certain subject.
9. Younger students need basic P.D.E.M.s if they are to be motivated in the proper direction.
10. A few general P.D.E.M.s to increase learning interest are:
    (1) Knowledge is power.
    (2) The more you learn, including subjects you don't like, the more you can help others.
    (3) Show how unliked subjects are related to subjects which are interesting.
    (4) Relate the unliked subjects to living situations.
11. Four self-hypnosis suggestions appealing to mental imagery are given: the sponge, the camera, the tape-recorder, and the electronic computer.
12. Examination freeze is a problem to many students.
13. Try to determine why you freeze during examination.
14. Self-hypnosis suggestion is given which will help you overcome examination freeze.
15. A six point plan is given to improve your concentration and memory.

18

CONCLUSION
"THE FUTURE IS YOURS"

WHAT DOES THE FUTURE HOLD for you? No mortal being can give a full and complete answer to this question. There are too many variables and uncertainties involved. Only God knows the absolute about the future, and some theologians would even argue this point. Even though you cannot predict the future, you can do certain things to insure your future. You cannot insure your future against sickness, accident, calamity, death, etc., but you can insure yourself a confident future. The future of the world cannot be controlled by you, but to a degree you can control some of the events which will take place in your life. Above all, you can control your attitude and outlook on life so you can live confidently in any circumstances life might hold for you. All things come alike to all men, but all men do not respond alike to "all things." Paul and Silas, in prison with bloody backs, sang praises to God and prayed at the midnight hour. John Bunyan wrote the immortal *Pilgrim's Progress* while confined in prison. Lesser men would have become disillusioned and broken in spirit.

Remember, what you do today determines, to a great extent, what your tomorrow will be. Self-hypnosis can help you build a strong, positive, realistic, action faith which will go with you into the future. Here are a few guide-lines you can use to build your future confidence.

1. *Check your foundation.* You are building a life, a character and a future. What kind of foundation are you building upon? Is it frail and faulty or is it strong and durable? If your life is built upon hatred, falsehood, and deceit it will someday crumble all around you. If it is built on truth, faith, and love it will endure. Build your life on these three things: truth, faith, and love. Never be afraid of the truth. Never be afraid to believe in that which is true. And never be afraid to love your God and your neighbor as yourself.

No matter how beautiful your life or character might appear on the surface, it will be destroyed by the winds of adversity if you have a weak foundation. If the foundation of your life is weak and insufficient, start immediately to construct a new one.

2. *Build consistently.* One feather doesn't weigh very much, but if you add other feathers every day, you will eventually have a load of feathers you can't lift. Even so with your life. One bit of knowledge isn't a lot, but if you consistently add to that one bit of knowledge you will someday be a very informed person. One act of faith might not seem like very much, but if you compound it daily with other deeds of faith, you will soon have a tremendous amount of faith, and remember, a faith like a grain of mustard seed can perform miracles. Consistent action pays off. The world is looking for men and women who can be depended upon. Be that person!

3. *Solidify your gains in life.* If you burn your bridges behind you, be sure to leave a rope you can swing back on. Some day you might need to go back. As much as possible keep all the friends you make. Retain all the knowledge you have acquired as fresh in your mind as possible. Because you aren't using something today doesn't mean you won't be using it tomorrow. Conserve what you construct.

4. *Follow through. Finish what you begin.* That is, if it is worth finishing. So many people jump from one task to another without finishing anything. If you finish something today, it will be ready for you tomorrow.

5. *Begin today to apply the teachings of this book to your life.* Believe in yourself and your future. You can live confidently and meet the demands of fulfilled living in the space age through the application of self-hypnosis.

A PERSONAL WORD FROM MELVIN POWERS, PUBLISHER, WILSHIRE BOOK COMPANY

My goal is to publish interesting, informative, and inspirational books. You can help me to accomplish this by sending me your answers to the following questions:

Did you enjoy reading this book? Why?

What ideas in the book impressed you most? Have you applied them to your daily life? How?

Is there a chapter that could serve as a theme for an entire book? Explain.

Would you like to read similar books? What additional information would you like them to contain?

If you have an idea for a book, I would welcome discussing it with you. If you have a manuscript in progress, write or call me concerning possible publication.

Melvin Powers
12015 Sherman Road
North Hollywood, California 91605

(818) 765-8579

MELVIN POWERS SELF-IMPROVEMENT LIBRARY

ASTROLOGY
____ASTROLOGY—HOW TO CHART YOUR HOROSCOPE Max Heindel 7.00
____ASTROLOGY AND SEXUAL ANALYSIS Morris C. Goodman 10.00
____ASTROLOGY AND YOU Carroll Righter 5.00
____ASTROLOGY MADE EASY Astarte 7.00
____ASTROLOGY, ROMANCE, YOU AND THE STARS Anthony Norvell 10.00
____MY WORLD OF ASTROLOGY Sydney Omarr 10.00
____THOUGHT DIAL Sydney Omarr 7.00
____WHAT THE STARS REVEAL ABOUT THE MEN IN YOUR LIFE Thelma White 3.00

BRIDGE
____BRIDGE BIDDING MADE EASY Edwin B. Kantar 15.00
____BRIDGE CONVENTIONS Edwin B. Kantar 10.00
____COMPETITIVE BIDDING IN MODERN BRIDGE Edgar Kaplan 7.00
____DEFENSIVE BRIDGE PLAY COMPLETE Edwin B Kantar 20.00
____GAMESMAN BRIDGE—PLAY BETTER WITH KANTAR Edwin B. Kantar 7.00
____HOW TO IMPROVE YOUR BRIDGE Alfred Sheinwold 7.00
____IMPROVING YOUR BIDDING SKILLS Edwin B. Kantar 10.00
____INTRODUCTION TO DECLARER'S PLAY Edwin B. Kantar 10.00
____INTRODUCTION TO DEFENDER'S PLAY Edwin B. Kantar 10.00
____KANTAR FOR THE DEFENSE Edwin B. Kantar 10.00
____KANTAR FOR THE DEFENSE VOLUME 2 Edwin B. Kantar 10.00
____TEST YOUR BRIDGE PLAY Edwin B. Kantar 10.00
____VOLUME 2—TEST YOUR BRIDGE PLAY Edwin B. Kantar 10.00
____WINNING DECLARER PLAY Dorothy Hayden Truscott 10.00

BUSINESS, STUDY & REFERENCE
____BRAINSTORMING Charles Clark 10.00
____CONVERSATION MADE EASY Elliot Russell 5.00
____EXAM SECRET Dennis B. Jackson 7.00
____FIX-IT BOOK Arthur Symons 2.00
____HOW TO DEVELOP A BETTER SPEAKING VOICE M. Hellier 5.00
____HOW TO SAVE 50% ON GAS & CAR EXPENSES Ken Stansbie 5.00
____HOW TO SELF-PUBLISH YOUR BOOK & MAKE IT A BEST SELLER Melvin Powers .. 20.00
____INCREASE YOUR LEARNING POWER Geoffrey A. Dudley 5.00
____PRACTICAL GUIDE TO BETTER CONCENTRATION Melvin Powers 5.00
____PUBLIC SPEAKING MADE EASY Thomas Montalbo 10.00
____7 DAYS TO FASTER READING William S. Schaill 7.00
____SONGWRITER'S RHYMING DICTIONARY Jane Shaw Whitfield 10.00
____SPELLING MADE EASY Lester D. Basch & Dr. Milton Finkelstein 3.00
____STUDENT'S GUIDE TO BETTER GRADES J.A. Rickard 3.00
____YOUR WILL & WHAT TO DO ABOUT IT Attorney Samuel G. King 7.00

CALLIGRAPHY
____ADVANCED CALLIGRAPHY Katherine Jeffares 7.00
____CALLIGRAPHY—THE ART OF BEAUTIFUL WRITING Katherine Jeffares 7.00
____CALLIGRAPHY FOR FUN & PROFIT Anne Leptich & Jacque Evans 10.00
____CALLIGRAPHY MADE EASY Tina Serafini 7.00

CHESS & CHECKERS
____BEGINNER'S GUIDE TO WINNING CHESS Fred Reinfeld 10.00
____CHESS IN TEN EASY LESSONS Larry Evans 10.00
____CHESS MADE EASY Milton L. Hanauer 5.00
____CHESS PROBLEMS FOR BEGINNERS Edited by Fred Reinfeld 7.00
____CHESS TACTICS FOR BEGINNERS Edited by Fred Reinfeld 10.00
____HOW TO WIN AT CHECKERS Fred Reinfeld 7.00

_____ 1001 BRILLIANT WAYS TO CHECKMATE Fred Reinfeld 10.00
_____ 1001 WINNING CHESS SACRIFICES & COMBINATIONS Fred Reinfeld 10.00

COOKERY & HERBS
_____ CULPEPER'S HERBAL REMEDIES Dr. Nicholas Culpeper 5.00
_____ FAST GOURMET COOKBOOK Poppy Cannon 2.50
_____ HEALING POWER OF HERBS May Bethel 5.00
_____ HEALING POWER OF NATURAL FOODS May Bethel 7.00
_____ HERBS FOR HEALTH—HOW TO GROW & USE THEM Louise Evans Doole 7.00
_____ HOME GARDEN COOKBOOK—DELICIOUS NATURAL FOOD RECIPES Ken Kraft 3.00
_____ MEATLESS MEAL GUIDE Tomi Ryan & James H. Ryan, M.D. 4.00
_____ VEGETABLE GARDENING FOR BEGINNERS Hugh Wilberg 2.00
_____ VEGETABLES FOR TODAY'S GARDENS R. Milton Carleton 2.00
_____ VEGETARIAN COOKERY Janet Walker 10.00
_____ VEGETARIAN COOKING MADE EASY & DELECTABLE Veronica Vezza 3.00

GAMBLING & POKER
_____ HOW TO WIN AT POKER Terence Reese & Anthony T. Watkins 10.00
_____ SCARNE ON DICE John Scarne 15.00
_____ WINNING AT CRAPS Dr. Lloyd T. Commins 10.00
_____ WINNING AT GIN Chester Wander & Cy Rice 10.00
_____ WINNING AT POKER—AN EXPERT'S GUIDE John Archer 10.00
_____ WINNING AT 21—AN EXPERT'S GUIDE John Archer 10.00
_____ WINNING POKER SYSTEMS Norman Zadeh 10.00

HEALTH
_____ BEE POLLEN Lynda Lyngheim & Jack Scagnetti 5.00
_____ COPING WITH ALZHEIMER'S Rose Oliver, Ph.D. & Francis Bock, Ph.D. 10.00
_____ DR. LINDNER'S POINT SYSTEM FOOD PROGRAM Peter G Lindner, M.D. 2.00
_____ HELP YOURSELF TO BETTER SIGHT Margaret Darst Corbett 7.00
_____ HOW YOU CAN STOP SMOKING PERMANENTLY Ernest Caldwell 5.00
_____ MIND OVER PLATTER Peter G Lindner, M.D. 5.00
_____ NATURE'S WAY TO NUTRITION & VIBRANT HEALTH Robert J. Scrutton 3.00
_____ NEW CARBOHYDRATE DIET COUNTER Patti Lopez-Pereira 2.00
_____ REFLEXOLOGY Dr. Maybelle Segal 7.00
_____ REFLEXOLOGY FOR GOOD HEALTH Anna Kaye & Don C. Matchan 10.00
_____ 30 DAYS TO BEAUTIFUL LEGS Dr. Marc Selner 3.00
_____ YOU CAN LEARN TO RELAX Dr. Samuel Gutwirth 5.00

HOBBIES
_____ BEACHCOMBING FOR BEGINNERS Norman Hickin 2.00
_____ BLACKSTONE'S MODERN CARD TRICKS Harry Blackstone 7.00
_____ BLACKSTONE'S SECRETS OF MAGIC Harry Blackstone 7.00
_____ COIN COLLECTING FOR BEGINNERS Burton Hobson & Fred Reinfeld 7.00
_____ ENTERTAINING WITH ESP Tony 'Doc' Shiels 2.00
_____ 400 FASCINATING MAGIC TRICKS YOU CAN DO Howard Thurston 7.00
_____ HOW I TURN JUNK INTO FUN AND PROFIT Sari 3.00
_____ HOW TO WRITE A HIT SONG AND SELL IT Tommy Boyce 10.00
_____ MAGIC FOR ALL AGES Walter Gibson 10.00
_____ PLANTING A TREE TreePeople with Andy & Katie Lipkis 13.00
_____ STAMP COLLECTING FOR BEGINNERS Burton Hobson 3.00

HORSE PLAYERS' WINNING GUIDES
_____ BETTING HORSES TO WIN Les Conklin 10.00
_____ ELIMINATE THE LOSERS Bob McKnight 5.00
_____ HOW TO PICK WINNING HORSES Bob McKnight 5.00
_____ HOW TO WIN AT THE RACES Sam (The Genius) Lewin 5.00
_____ HOW YOU CAN BEAT THE RACES Jack Kavanagh 5.00
_____ MAKING MONEY AT THE RACES David Barr 7.00

MELVIN POWERS MAIL ORDER LIBRARY

___ HOW TO GET RICH IN MAIL ORDER Melvin Powers 20.00
___ HOW TO SELF-PUBLISH YOUR BOOK Melvin Powers 20.00
___ HOW TO WRITE A GOOD ADVERTISEMENT Victor O. Schwab 20.00
___ MAIL ORDER MADE EASY J. Frank Brumbaugh 20.00
___ MAKING MONEY WITH CLASSIFIED ADS Melvin Powers 20.00

METAPHYSICS & NEW AGE

___ CONCENTRATION—A GUIDE TO MENTAL MASTERY Mouni Sadhu 10.00
___ EXTRA-TERRESTRIAL INTELLIGENCE—THE FIRST ENCOUNTER 6.00
___ FORTUNE TELLING WITH CARDS P. Foli 10.00
___ HOW TO INTERPRET DREAMS, OMENS & FORTUNE TELLING SIGNS Gettings 5.00
___ HOW TO UNDERSTAND YOUR DREAMS Geoffrey A. Dudley 7.00
___ MAGICIAN—HIS TRAINING AND WORK W.E. Butler 7.00
___ MEDITATION Mouni Sadhu 10.00
___ MODERN NUMEROLOGY Morris C. Goodman 5.00
___ NUMEROLOGY—ITS FACTS AND SECRETS Ariel Yvon Taylor 5.00
___ NUMEROLOGY MADE EASY W. Mykian 5.00
___ PALMISTRY MADE EASY Fred Gettings 7.00
___ PALMISTRY MADE PRACTICAL Elizabeth Daniels Squire 7.00
___ PROPHECY IN OUR TIME Martin Ebon 2.50
___ SUPERSTITION—ARE YOU SUPERSTITIOUS? Eric Maple 2.00
___ TAROT OF THE BOHEMIANS Papus 10.00
___ WAYS TO SELF-REALIZATION Mouni Sadhu 7.00
___ WITCHCRAFT, MAGIC & OCCULTISM—A FASCINATING HISTORY W.B. Crow 10.00
___ WITCHCRAFT—THE SIXTH SENSE Justine Glass 7.00

RECOVERY

___ KNIGHT IN RUSTY ARMOR Robert Fisher 5.00
___ KNIGHT IN RUSTY ARMOR (Hard cover edition) Robert Fisher 10.00
___ KNIGHTS WITHOUT ARMOR (Hard cover edition) Aaron R. Kipnis, Ph.D. 10.00
___ PRINCESS WHO BELIEVED IN FAIRY TALES Marcia Grad 10.00

SELF-HELP & INSPIRATIONAL

___ CHANGE YOUR VOICE, CHANGE YOUR LIFE Morton Cooper, Ph.D. 10.00
___ CHARISMA—HOW TO GET "THAT SPECIAL MAGIC" Marcia Grad 10.00
___ DAILY POWER FOR JOYFUL LIVING Dr. Donald Curtis 7.00
___ DYNAMIC THINKING Melvin Powers 5.00
___ GREATEST POWER IN THE UNIVERSE U.S. Andersen 10.00
___ GROW RICH WHILE YOU SLEEP Ben Sweetland 10.00
___ GROW RICH WITH YOUR MILLION DOLLAR MIND Brian Adams 7.00
___ GROWTH THROUGH REASON Albert Ellis, Ph.D. 10.00
___ GUIDE TO PERSONAL HAPPINESS Albert Ellis, Ph.D. & Irving Becker, Ed.D. 10.00
___ GUIDE TO RATIONAL LIVING Albert Ellis, Ph.D. & R. Harper, Ph.D. 15.00
___ HANDWRITING ANALYSIS MADE EASY John Marley 10.00
___ HANDWRITING TELLS Nadya Olyanova 10.00
___ HOW TO ATTRACT GOOD LUCK A.H.Z. Carr 10.00
___ HOW TO DEVELOP A WINNING PERSONALITY Martin Panzer 10.00
___ HOW TO DEVELOP AN EXCEPTIONAL MEMORY Young & Gibson 10.00
___ HOW TO LIVE WITH A NEUROTIC Albert Ellis, Ph.D. 10.00
___ HOW TO MAKE $100,000 A YEAR IN SALES Albert Winnikoff 15.00
___ HOW TO OVERCOME YOUR FEARS M.P. Leahy, M.D. 3.00
___ HOW TO SUCCEED Brian Adams 10.00
___ HUMAN PROBLEMS & HOW TO SOLVE THEM Dr. Donald Curtis 5.00
___ I CAN Ben Sweetland 10.00
___ I WILL Ben Sweetland 10.00
___ KNIGHT IN RUSTY ARMOR Robert Fisher 5.00
___ KNIGHT IN RUSTY ARMOR (Hard Cover) Robert Fisher 10.00
___ MAGIC IN YOUR MIND U.S. Andersen 15.00

____MAGIC OF THINKING SUCCESS Dr. David J. Schwartz 10.00
____MAGIC POWER OF YOUR MIND Walter M. Germain 10.00
____NEVER UNDERESTIMATE THE SELLING POWER OF A WOMAN Dottie Walters 7.00
____PRINCESS WHO BELIEVED IN FAIRY TALES Marcia Grad 10.00
____PSYCHO-CYBERNETICS Maxwell Maltz, M.D. 10.00
____PSYCHOLOGY OF HANDWRITING Nadya Olyanova 10.00
____SALES CYBERNETICS Brian Adams 10.00
____SECRET OF SECRETS U.S. Andersen 10.00
____SECRET POWER OF THE PYRAMIDS U.S. Andersen 7.00
____SELF-THERAPY FOR THE STUTTERER Malcolm Frazer 3.00
____STOP COMMITTING VOICE SUICIDE Morton Cooper, Ph.D. 10.00
____SUCCESS CYBERNETICS U.S. Andersen 10.00
____10 DAYS TO A GREAT NEW LIFE William E. Edwards 3.00
____THINK AND GROW RICH Napoleon Hill 10.00
____THINK LIKE A WINNER Walter Doyle Staples, Ph.D. 15.00
____THREE MAGIC WORDS U.S. Andersen 12.00
____TREASURY OF COMFORT Edited by Rabbi Sidney Greenberg 10.00
____TREASURY OF THE ART OF LIVING Edited by Rabbi Sidney Greenberg ... 10.00
____WHAT YOUR HANDWRITING REVEALS Albert E. Hughes 4.00
____WINNING WITH YOUR VOICE Morton Cooper, Ph.D. 10.00
____WONDER WITHIN Thomas F. Coyle, M.D. 10.00
____YOUR SUBCONSCIOUS POWER Charles M. Simmons 7.00

SPORTS
____BILLIARDS—POCKET • CAROM • THREE CUSHION Clive Cottingham, Jr. 10.00
____COMPLETE GUIDE TO FISHING Vlad Evanoff 2.00
____HOW TO IMPROVE YOUR RACQUETBALL Lubarsky, Kaufman & Scagnetti 5.00
____HOW TO WIN AT POCKET BILLIARDS Edward D. Knuchell 10.00
____JOY OF WALKING Jack Scagnetti 3.00
____RACQUETBALL FOR WOMEN Toni Hudson, Jack Scagnetti & Vince Rondone 3.00
____SECRET OF BOWLING STRIKES Dawson Taylor 5.00
____SOCCER—THE GAME & HOW TO PLAY IT Gary Rosenthal 7.00
____STARTING SOCCER Edward F Dolan, Jr. 5.00

TENNIS LOVERS' LIBRARY
____HOW TO BEAT BETTER TENNIS PLAYERS Loring Fiske 4.00
____PSYCH YOURSELF TO BETTER TENNIS Dr. Walter A. Luszki 2.00
____TENNIS FOR BEGINNERS Dr. H.A. Murray 2.00
____WEEKEND TENNIS—HOW TO HAVE FUN & WIN AT THE SAME TIME Bill Talbert ... 3.00

WILSHIRE PET LIBRARY
____DOG TRAINING MADE EASY & FUN John W. Kellogg 5.00
____HOW TO BRING UP YOUR PET DOG Kurt Unkelbach 2.00
____HOW TO RAISE & TRAIN YOUR PUPPY Jeff Griffen 5.00

Available from your bookstore or directly from Melvin Powers.
Please add $2.00 shipping and handling for each book ordered.

Melvin Powers
12015 Sherman Road, No. Hollywood, California 91605

For our complete catalog, visit our Web site at http://www.mpowers.com.

WILSHIRE HORSE LOVERS' LIBRARY

Available from your bookstore or directly from Melvin Powers.
Please add $2.00 shipping and handling for each book ordered.

Melvin Powers

12015 Sherman Road, No. Hollywood, California 91605

For our complete catalog, visit our Web site at http://www.mpowers.com.

Books by Melvin Powers

HOW TO GET RICH IN MAIL ORDER

1. How to Develop Your Mail Order Expertise 2. How to Find a Unique Product or Service to Sell 3. How to Make Money with Classified Ads 4. How to Make Money with Display Ads 5. The Unlimited Potential for Making Money with Direct Mail 6. How to Copycat Successful Mail Order Operations 7. How I Created a Bestseller Using the Copycat Technique 8. How to Start and Run a Profitable Mail Order Special Interest Book Business 9. I Enjoy Selling Books by Mail—Some of My Successful Ads 10. Five of My Most Successful Direct Mail Pieces That Sold and Are Selling Millions of Dollars' Worth of Books 11. Melvin Powers's Mail Order Success Strategy—Follow it and You'll Become a Millionaire 12. How to Sell Your Products to Mail Order Companies, Retail Outlets, Jobbers, and Fund Raisers for Maximum Distribution and Profit 13. How to Get Free Display Ads and Publicity that Will Put You on the Road to Riches 14. How to Make Your Advertising Copy Sizzle 15. Questions and Answers to Help You Get Started Making Money 16. A Personal Word from Melvin Powers 17. How to Get Started 18. Selling Products on Television   8½" x 11½" — 352 Pages . . . $20.00

MAKING MONEY WITH CLASSIFIED ADS

1. Getting Started with Classified Ads 2. Everyone Loves to Read Classified Ads 3. How to Find a Money-Making Product 4. How to Write Classified Ads that Make Money 5. What I've Learned from Running Thousands of Classified Ads 6. Classified Ads Can Help You Make Big Money in Multi-Level Programs 7. Two-Step Classified Ads Made Me a Multi-Millionaire—They Can Do the Same for You! 8. One-Inch Display Ads Can Work Wonders 9. Display Ads Can Make You a Fortune Overnight 10. Although I Live in California, I Buy My Grapefruit from Florida 11. Nuts and Bolts of Mail Order Success 12. What if You Can't Get Your Business Running Successfully? What's Wrong? How to Correct it 13. Strategy for Mail Order Success   8½" x 11½" — 240 Pages . . . $20.00

HOW TO SELF-PUBLISH YOUR BOOK AND HAVE THE FUN AND EXCITEMENT OF BEING A BEST-SELLING AUTHOR

1. Who is Melvin Powers? 2. What is the Motivation Behind Your Decision to Publish Your Book? 3. Why You Should Read This Chapter Even if You Already Have an Idea for a Book 4. How to Test the Salability of Your Book Before You Write One Word 5. How I Achieved Sales Totaling $2,000,000 on My Book *How to Get Rich in Mail Order* 6. How to Develop a Second Career by Using Your Expertise 7. How to Choose an Enticing Book Title 8. Marketing Strategy 9. Success Stories 10. How to Copyright Your Book 11. How to Write a Winning Advertisement 12. Advertising that Money Can't Buy 13. Questions and Answers to Help You Get Started 14. Self-Publishing and the Midas Touch
8½" x 11½" — 240 Pages . . . $20.00

A PRACTICAL GUIDE TO SELF-HYPNOSIS

1. What You Should Know about Self-Hypnosis 2. What about the Dangers of Hypnosis? 3. Is Hypnosis the Answer? 4. How Does Self-Hypnosis Work? 5. How to Arouse Yourself From the Self-Hypnotic State 6. How to Attain Self-Hypnosis 7. Deepening the Self-Hypnotic State 8. What You Should Know about Becoming an Excellent Subject 9. Techniques for Reaching the Somnambulistic State 10. A New Approach to Self-Hypnosis 11. Psychological Aids and Their Function 12. Practical Applications of Self-Hypnosis
144 Pages . . . $10.00

Available at your bookstore or directly from Melvin Powers.
Please add $2.00 shipping and handling for each book ordered.

Melvin Powers
12015 Sherman Road, No. Hollywood, California 91605

For our complete catalog, visit our Web site at http://www.mpowers.com.

NOTES